Growing Roses

JOHN MATTOCK

Photographs by Deni Bown

WARD LOCK

First published in Great Britain in 1993
by Ward Lock Limited, Villiers House, 41/47 Strand,
London WC2N 5JE, England
A Cassell Imprint

British Library Cataloguing in Publication Data is
available upon application to the British Library

ISBN 0 7063 7132 1

Text filmset by Litho Link Ltd, Welshpool, Powys
Printed and bound in Singapore by Craft Print Pte Ltd

Previous page: **'Lovers'
Meeting', an extremely
healthy orange-tangerine
rose which positively glows
in the border and is useful
for cutting.**

Contents

Preface

The rose has no equal in popularity as a garden plant. Wherever it is possible to grow temperate-loving plants, the rose has been the gardener's favourite. Because of its immense popularity many fables and fallacies have become associated with it. This book has been written to demonstrate that the world's most popular flower is not difficult to grow and a good sensible approach will produce a continuity of flower and a high degree of beauty.

In legends throughout time the rose has been a symbol of love and fidelity. Even 2000 years ago mystique had been built up surrounding its properties and significance, giving it huge symbolic value in civilized communities. Originally adopted as a source of medicinal properties, it quickly became fashionable. A curious fact which is un-typical of a plant that has been domesticated for so long is that it is not mentioned in the New Testament.

Historically the rose was developed during the progress of two civilizations in Europe and the Far East. The conflux of varieties from these two quite disparate geographical areas gave a meaningful purpose to the development of the rose as we know it today. There were no roses growing in western Europe that flowered after mid-summer (or were recurrent flowering). Similarly, notwithstanding the rather romantic concepts of painters, rambling roses did not exist in western gardens before 1750 AD.

As an art form artists have sought to exemplify the beauty of the rose, epitomized by the well known contributions of Redoubté to the present day.

Attar of roses, the essential ingredient of many scents, is still a major contributor to the national income of at least one central European province. Wines and conserves are still contributing to the kitchen, and rosehip syrup is alleged to be an essential source of vitamin C.

As a garden plant it has been developed out of all recognition to become an asset that provides colour and pleasure anywhere, from the largest gardens to the smallest garden patio. Many fallacies have inevitably arisen with its popularity, many unfortunately to its detriment. Contrary to common assumption, it will grow in the majority of soils. It may require an annual prune but not in the ritualistic form that many would have us think. There is as much scent in the modern rose as there ever has been. Disease resistance is greater now than ever before. The colour range is quite incredible and new shapes and forms are being developed every year.

Common sense is the criteria with everything in the garden. If liberties are taken then a rose, like other plants, will object and reject its owners. On the other hand, if it is sensibly fed and grown in appropriate situations, it will give a lifetime of pleasure and romance.   J.M.

◄ *Rosa* 'Raubritter' (*macrantha* ×), a perfectly shaped plant which produces a mound of cup-shaped silvery-pink flowers in mid-summer.

AUTHOR'S ACKNOWLEDGEMENTS

The author would like to acknowledge the valuable contribution of Lieutenant Colonel K. Grapes, the Secretary of the Royal National Rose Society, and Mrs Jill Bennell, the Secretary of the World Federation of Rose Societies.

PUBLISHER'S ACKNOWLEDGEMENTS

The colour photographs in this book were taken by Deni Bown, apart from the following: pages 16 (bottom), 32, 37, 56, 57 and 73 were reproduced by kind permission of John Mattock, and page 93 was taken by Clive Nichols.

The line illustrations were drawn by David Woodroffe.

· 1 ·

Types of Roses

Gardening has been a pastime and mark of civilization since time began. With changing ideas and a new social awareness, the rich man has been unable to maintain a fleet of gardeners and the poor man has risen above the necessity to grow vegetables to the exclusion of ornamental plants. The culture of the rose is no longer the prerogative of the professional gardener. It is now much easier to grow and there are many knowledgeable experts willing to give helpful advice.

Rose breeders have been in the forefront of developing our national flower to accommodate every conceivable situation in the garden. Whether it be a screen to give privacy to a plot, or a cut flower to provide pleasure for the housebound, there is a rose for all situations.

BUSH ROSES (Fig. 1)

Hybrid tea

By far and away the most popular type of rose, the Hybrid tea is the greatest product of the rose breeders' art. A beautiful bloom of classical form, with characteristic reflexed petals, it is a far cry from the *eglantine* of Shakespeare's sonnets. The Hybrid tea is defined as a large-flowered rose borne singly on stems and epitomized by the most popular rose of all time, 'Peace'. True that bush roses of this type will sometimes produce clusters, but the lateral growths are inferior and many gardeners remove them. (This is called dis-budding.) They range in height from 60 cm to 1.2 m (2–4 ft) and with judicious pruning will provide bloom from early summer to midautumn. In many mild climates they will grow even taller. Their colour range is now truly wide ranging, but in common with all types of rose will always be at their best in full sunlight.

Hybrid tea roses will look their best in formal rose beds but such criteria is not mandatory and they can be planted in mixed herbaceous and shrub borders. They will respond to good balanced feeding and are not demanding, although like most plants they will not thrive on neglect.

● *Scent* Much has been made of the cliché that roses do not have the scent of yesteryear and it is unfortunate that this assumption still prevails. Though it would be true of many varieties introduced 60 years ago, today virtually all Hybrid tea roses possess some scent, and a considerable number have perfume which surpasses the headiest fragrance possessed by their ancestors.

● *Disease* Much has also been made of the Hybrid tea rose's vulnerability to disease. It is true to say that certain breeding lines did produce a legacy of proneness to the vigours of life but rose breeders can now be proud of their progeny and without doubt there is greater resistance than at any other time. If the inexperienced gardener persists in growing his roses in a draught, in waterlogged beds or in association with some of the older disease-carriers, he is an optimist.

Hybrid tea bush roses have set a standard for quality both as a garden plant and as a cut flower which no other genus of plant has ever equalled, let alone surpassed.

Floribunda

Imagine a Hybrid tea bush rose, but with a cluster of blooms and no disbudding. Alternatively, a bush rose throwing a cluster of blooms, with no bloom any bigger than another. That in short is the definition of a Floribunda. Of relatively recent introduction and development, they have progressed from the early Poulsen roses, to the post-war years of Hybrid Polyanthas, to the present day nomenclature.

The modern cluster-flowered rose, the Floribunda, has all the attributes of its slightly more sophisticated cousin, the Hybrid tea, without the large blooms associated with the latter. They have a history of being somewhat more robust and thriving in more rugged circumstances, which may have been relevant when the earlier Hybrid teas were temperamental and required greater care. They also had the reputation of requiring less protection and slightly less vigorous pruning.

Today many of the early presumptions about Floribundas have been discarded and the knowledgeable gardener assumes a cultural similarity in all respects to a Hybrid tea. So what is the difference? Simply, does the gardener want large blooms borne singly on a stem, or is he demanding flower power and a mass of bloom irrespective of size? It is quite incorrect for a bush rose to be listed as either a Hybrid tea or a Floribunda. What can sometimes happen is that a poorly grown Floribunda will produce single blooms and occasionally a Hybrid tea will be over enthusiastic and throw big clusters. This is a symptom of poor nomenclature and the demand from tidy minds that all plants should be pigeon-holed when catalogued. For sheer continuity of flower and blaze of colour, the Floribunda has no equal. Cultural and physical demands are precisely those of the Hybrid teas. So why the difference? In truth very little. If the plant is a cluster with all its blooms of equal merit then it is a Floribunda, whereas an Hybrid tea has a dominant bloom and the laterals are of no significance. It could well be argued that the height range of a Floribunda is much greater, from 60 cm–1.8 m (2–6 ft) but that is *in extremis*. Many would suggest that Floribundas do not have the scent of some Hybrid teas, which is probably true but it is more than compensated by the sheer mass of flower which has no equal among bedding plants.

STANDARDS (Fig. 2)

Any variety of rose in cultivation can be grown as a standard but not every rose will make a good standard. So what is a standard? The majority of garden roses do not grow on their own roots; they are budded (propagated) on a rootstock. This simple exercise provides a plant with a greater virility and an enhanced quality of bloom. A standard rose is simply any variety that is propagated on a stem somewhere between 60 cm and 1.8 m (2 ft and 6 ft) from ground level. In many gardens they may appear incongruous but in others, particularly formal plantings, the complement of colour at a raised height can give life to an otherwise meaningless bed. However, because of this height they are prone to wind damage. You need to consider carefully their planting position and ensure they are very well staked.

'Silver Jubilee' is the biggest selling Hybrid tea on the British market. An extremely free-flowering pink with salmon undertones and disease-resistant foliage.

Hybrid tea and Floribunda standards

Although in theory every rose can be propagated as a standard, in practice this is not true. Firstly, not every variety makes a good head. The really vigorous varieties like 'Alexander' or the Queen Elizabeth rose are very ugly as standards. Secondly, occasionally an extremely successful bush rose variety will not grow on a standard. Little is known about this phenomenon but fortunately the nurseries will have discovered this before it occurs in gardens.

Half standards

Half standards are available and some of the newer patio and miniature roses propagated this way make an admirable show in small gardens. The height of a normal standard is measured from ground level to the first propagated shoot. The generally accepted height for a full standard is 1 m (3¼ ft). Half standards can be as short as 30 cm (1 ft), but a more common height is 75 cm (2½ ft).

Fig. 1 Standard roses.

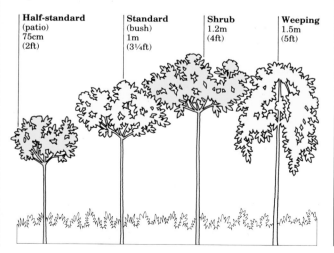

Half-standard (patio) 75cm (2ft)	Standard (bush) 1m (3¼ft)	Shrub 1.2m (4ft)	Weeping 1.5m (5ft)

Shrub standards

The introduction of the newer ground-cover roses has expanded the types that are available under this general title. Nevertheless, the older shrubs 'The Fairy' and 'Ballerina' have become very popular and make a valuable contribution to gardens round the world. They are all recurrent.

Weeping standards

By far the most dramatic form of standard, the 'umbrella' rose in full flower, is a show stopper. In reality they are rambling roses budded at about 1.5 m (5 ft) requiring very strong staking and, although amazingly spectacular, have a very short flowering season.

PATIO ROSES

In the modern world the patio rose can best be described as the designer rose of the twentieth century. A patio rose is a short-growing Floribunda or, alternatively, a vigorous miniature. They share the longevity of the former with the characteristic small flower and foliage of the latter. They make ideal material for cultivation in a pot or tub. One or two throw the occasional tall shoots but the majority are perfectly formed 'miniature shrubs'.

MINIATURE ROSES

The species *Rosa rouletii* was discovered at the turn of the century. Selective hybridizing has produced a plant about 15–30 cm (6–12 in) high with perfectly shaped miniature blooms and foliage to match. Its very short stature has encouraged it to be grown as an alpine, to which it is certainly not suited, resulting in a short life span. Miniature roses are probably happier grown in special areas in the garden where they have no competition.

OLD GARDEN ROSES

The old garden roses, or heritage roses, cover a time span from the introduction of cultivated roses to the advent of the modern rose which occurred some 150 years ago. As civilization developed, so did the appreciation of the rose, particularly in western Europe. In common with many other plants, they were cultivated for their herbal properties but quickly developed as house-

Fig. 2 Bush roses.

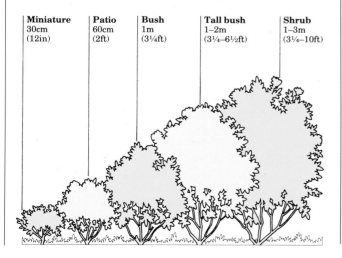

Miniature	Patio	Bush	Tall bush	Shrub
30cm	60cm	1m	1–2m	1–3m
(12in)	(2ft)	(3¼ft)	(3¼–6½ft)	(3¼–10ft)

holders improved their amenities beyond their door and landscaped their properties. From early Grecian times to the age of Empress Josephine they enhanced gardens with their floriferousness and scent. Until the late eighteenth century they were only summer flowering but with the introduction of the Chinas, remontancy (recurrent flowering) was an important and valuable characteristic. It is therefore convenient to divide these noble and free-flowering types into summer flowering and repeat flowering.

Summer flowering

● *The albas* are a very brief step away from the wild rose and are characterized by their pretty pale foliage and a colour range from the purist white to the palest pink. They make very useful shrubs, and historically are associated with the white rose of York.

● *The gallicas* have a cultural history reaching back to the Grecian and Persian eras and have large blooms ranging in colour from the deepest maroon to pale lilacs and pinks with the occasional stripe. Reputedly the red rose of Lancaster. The beautiful swathes of bloom are in abundance in mid-summer.

● *The centifolias* are the rose made popular by the painting school of the Old Dutch Masters and were used extensively as cut flowers, albeit for a brief period in early summer.

● *The moss roses* are naturally evolved from the centifolias which occurred as recently as the fifteenth century. The medium-sized double blooms flower in mid-summer in profusion, but the plants lack character and should be planted at the back of borders where they may be appreciated when in flower but are conveniently forgotten for the rest of the year.

'Mermaid', the most exquisite climber. The prominent yellow stamens lend distinction to large single blooms on a vigorous semi-evergreen plant.

Repeat flowering

● *The bourbon roses* were the first big break in the development of the modern rose. The probable result of a cross between the newly discovered recurrent-flowering China roses and the damasks. Typical large-flowered lax shrubs with a flower form that was popularized in Victorian embroidery. Many are practically thornless and have an exquisite scent.

● *The hybrid perpetuals* are the immediate predecessors of the modern Hybrid teas. Large – almost gross – blooms, mistakenly called cabbage roses, are supported on untidy straggling bushes.

MODERN SHRUBS

This group can well be described as the culmination of modern breeding to produce a large plant sometimes 3 m (10 ft) high; the majority are recurrent flowering. In short they are Floribundas that are not pruned. Apart from the proliferation of varieties that cannot be classified, there are two groups that can.

● *The hybrid musks* are true recurrent shrubs with clusters of medium-sized flowers. They are a product of the early 1900s, and the majority are scented.

● *The hybrid rugosas* are a progression from the species. Identified by the typical covering of small thorns and large leathery foliage, they are ideal for hedging but do not enjoy the same immunity to disease as the type.

SPECIE ROSES

The specie or wild roses have an appeal as a garden plant which is unique. They grow in abundance in our hedgerows in one form or another and can be obtained in many regions in the temperate zones of the northern hemisphere. They range from the common dog rose (*Rosa canina*) to the exotic-looking *Rosa moyesii* which is a native of the Himalayas and decorates our gardens with bright metallic-red flowers and a harvest of large flask-shaped hips in the autumn. Although a few can be traced as direct ancestors of the modern rose, the majority have unique characteristics. Suitable as specimen plants or planted in shrubberies, those producing hips in the autumn lend interest and colour to a dull border; others can give dramatic displays of colour in the spring or, equally welcome, subtle variations of foliage in the summer.

'Trumpeter', one of the shorter-growing Floribundas with bright vermilion clusters of medium-sized flowers which will add sparkle to a dull border.

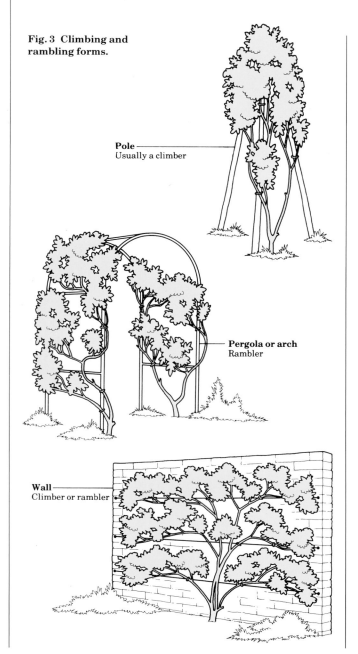

Fig. 3 Climbing and rambling forms.

Pole — Usually a climber

Pergola or arch Rambler

Wall — Climber or rambler

Specie roses must be allowed to grow naturally, without the necessity of pruning. A great advantage with them is that they give no problems in the matter of disease control.

CLIMBERS AND RAMBLERS (Fig. 3)

Walls covered in swathes of beautiful roses in early summer, arches and pergolas reminiscent of Victorian and Edwardian eras and festoons of colour smothering trees, the climbing and rambling roses have for the last 200 years graced many gardens, providing a feast of colour to herald the height of summer opulence.

The great debate has been on the difference between these two categories. A climbing rose is defined as a plant with growth that has the potential to cover walls and fences with the minimum of support – in other words, the plant structure is strong and upright, so it won't sprawl. On the other hand, a rambler is possessed of the same rapid growth but is lax in its stature and demands regular attention to secure it. Although it is generally assumed that climbers have large flowers, this is not usually so, as many climbers are mutations of bush varieties which can be either Hybrid teas or Floribundas. Ramblers by definition are not only lax in growth but also cluster flowered.

· LONG-LASTING FOLIAGE AND COLOUR ·

The rose is a deciduous plant. That means that it sheds its leaves at the end of the season in late autumn. There are nevertheless some varieties which keep their foliage for a very long time. They are all climbers or ramblers.

Name	Colour
'Félicité et Perpétue	White
'François Juranville'	Pink
'Mme Alfred Carrière'	White
'Mermaid'	Sulphur yellow
'Summer Wine'	Pink

The description 'continuous flowering' can be very misleading. Such roses do not exist, although there are a few which are extraordinarily recurrent.

Name	Colour
'Compassion'	Salmon
'Congratulations'	Pink
'Golden Showers'	Yellow
'Iceberg'	White
'Memento'	Pale vermilion
'Pink Pearl'	Pearl
'Selfridges'	Yellow
The Times Rose	Deep scarlet

Until recently, with one or two exceptions, they were all summer flowering. However, hybridists have now broken the mould and it is common today to describe climbers and ramblers by their flowering potential, i.e. climbing roses which are either summer flowering or recurrent; and rambling roses which are either summer flowering or recurrent.

Because of the difference in flower power, there is an inevitable difference in the rate of growth. A recurrent-flowering climber will cover a structure or support at a much slower rate and care must be taken to select the correct variety. All modern climbers are recurrent and do not have the vigour of their once-flowering counterparts. This lack of vigour is compensated by the bonus of a good showing of autumn flower.

GROUND-COVER ROSES (Fig. 4)

There are few plant genus that do not have a prostrate form and roses are no exception. As with many forms of ornamental horticulture, fashion is the mother of invention; only recently hybridists have applied their skills to producing a rose tailor-made for the environment. The criteria were very simple – a prostrate plant that required little or no maintenance (which obviously included no necessity to prune), a complete freedom from disease, and a harvest of flower that was continuous.

Many hybridists have attempted to achieve this with varying degrees of success. The first few were summer flowering and probably owed their existence to the old ramblers. Varieties were bred that grew at an extraordinary rate across the ground, and a single plant taking up to 9 sq m in two seasons was very common. Recently a more modified plant has been produced, spreading to just 1m or so (3–4 ft), with the invaluable attribute of recurrent flower.

Fig. 4 Ground cover shapes.

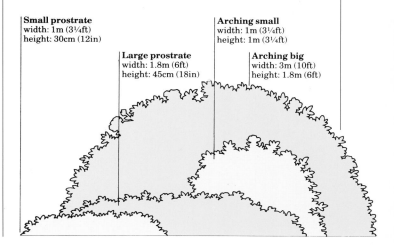

Small prostrate
width: 1m (3¼ft)
height: 30cm (12in)

Arching small
width: 1m (3¼ft)
height: 1m (3¼ft)

Large prostrate
width: 1.8m (6ft)
height: 45cm (18in)

Arching big
width: 3m (10ft)
height: 1.8m (6ft)

Small ground-cover roses are particularly ideal to clothe the top of small walls and difficult areas where the terrain does not lend itself to a more formal upright plant. The larger types are ideal to cover large banks and the green areas of urban conurbations to replace less exciting prostrate conifers.

ROSES INDOORS

Roses as cut flowers

For many rose lovers a spray of roses out of season is a token of love and respect. A modern cut-flower rose, of the type that is usually obtainable in a florist's shop, is the product of care and intense cultivation more often than not produced in a greenhouse or similarly protected environment. Specially bred and grown for this market, they are a world apart from the ordinary garden rose and very rarely will this type of plant thrive outside.

House plants

The rose is by nature a sun lover and is not at all happy in reduced light or an artificial environment. Recent progress in the development of pot roses has produced a presentable product, now obtainable in superstores and garden centres – a containerized plant which competes with many other house plants and all-year-round chrysanthemums. This type of rose will give pleasure for a short period but not indefinitely. They are grown in controlled conditions with protection, on their own roots, but will rarely be a success when planted in the garden.

◄ Top: 'Tuscany Superb', a popular Gallica whose scented dark purplish clusters and semi-lax plant style give distinction to an 'olde-worlde' border.

◄ Bottom: 'White Scotch', typical of the once popular *R. spinosissima* group which will thrive on the poorest of soils and are easily grown on their own roots.

· 2 ·
Roses in Design

Daydreaming, planning, planting – that is the pattern in planting any genus which contributes to the full enjoyment of a garden. The rose is not a terribly demanding plant in the garden, but it is well to pause and consider the venues and the type of rose which will fulfill the particular demands of the garden and the gardener. Does the plant have to climb? Will it produce a good shrub? Is it a good bedder? Can it scramble over a wall? There are many questions which the novice gardener will wish to ask. Catalogues may provide some of the answers but a visit to nurseries or large society gardens with information bureaux is a great help.

COLOUR CO-ORDINATION

Much is made of the acceptability of mixing colours in the garden. Will they blend or do they clash? Gardening is such a personal matter that it is difficult to be pedantic and produce profound statements on what or will not harmonize. The introduction of the more vivid vermilions in recent years did cause problems and there is no doubt that some pale pinks were ousted. Some colours can produce a jarring effect on the senses.

The most suitable foil for the very bright vermilions is scarlet. The cruder pinks are perhaps more difficult and can destroy the visual enjoyment of the pastel shades. White, which curiously is the most unpopular colour in roses, can be softened, if that is the right word, by introducing similar pale colours. The very deep crimsons are the most difficult colour to accommodate and can produce void areas.

SHAPES

A factor that is not often considered is the shape of a rose tree. The Queen Elizabeth Rose, a very tall statuesque plant, can contribute tremendously to the back of a border and provide colour to many drab situations; a miniature is a small round plant that suits a small patio.

Shapes are of great importance when considering the planning and disposition of shrubs and ground-cover roses.

Big round shrubs can act as specimen plants in parts of the garden that have been set aside for conservation purposes. the *rugosa* family does well in these situations.

Ground-cover roses have two distinct shapes. The flat spreading type are typified by the small 'Snow Carpet' or the sprawling 'Grouse', which will produce horizontal growth and can be utilized to grow over banks in a spectacular fashion. The arching types have a dome shape; they can well be described as suitable in large landscapes, and big borders, or alternatively disguising difficult areas in small gardens.

Shapes only present a problem with over enthusiasm for vigour. The Queen Elizabeth Rose, described as a Floribunda, can produce ugly effects because of its habit of leaving the gardener with a view of horrible lengths of green stem seemingly supporting bloom which is too high to be enjoyed. Fortunately there are few rose varieties with this problem.

ARCHES, PERGOLAS AND SCREENS

The concepts of roses gracing great arches and screens is steeped in the history of Victorian gardens, and curiously has altered very little in recent years – notwithstanding the tremendous advances that have been made in breeding new types and forms. The ability for any rose to clamber over fences and pergolas was made possible with the introduction of the *wichuraiana* and *multiflora* types from the Far East, collected by intrepid plant hunters. In a short space of time roses were available to climb and ramble in a most satisfactory way and, with one or two notable additions, it is the varieties that were introduced some 50 to 150 years ago which are the mainstay of garden design today.

The criteria are very simple. Roses that will grow very quickly, have the potential to scramble anywhere and will give pleasure for as long as possible. Fortunately the first two are very easy to obtain but the third has not been achieved. We therefore have to accept that really fast-growing ramblers and climbers will only flower for a short period in early to mid-summer. They are nonetheless a fantastic sight when well grown and well worth the effort to produce. By their very nature they are lax growers and therefore require ample support. On mainland Europe and many other parts of the world these are constructed with wrought iron but in the UK wood has proved much more successful. Care must be taken, when building this form of architecture, to treat the bases with some form of wood preservative which must be applied well before placement and allowed to dry out. This type of structure requires an annual inspection to avoid disappointment and disaster.

The range of varieties and colour in climbers and ramblers is considerable, but yellows are at a premium. Like all roses, judicous pruning will give good dividends but it is of greater importance to tie in new growth as it is produced, to avoid wind damage. There are a few exceptionally vigorous varieties that are ideal to climb through trees. Care must be taken to plant in a well-prepared position, as the soil under trees is very often of a poor quality. Nevertheless, with patience, amazing results can be obtained. Big old fruit trees which have to be preserved make an ideal framework for this concept, provided the fruit does not have to be picked – it's a thorny experience!

Walls are the providence of the slower-growing climbers, where fortunately the range of varieties can be extended to the modern recurrent introductions which will provide a longer season of bloom.

HEDGES

The rose is a gregarious plant that can be adapted to many positions in the garden and there is no greater sight than a colourful hedge of roses. They range in width and height relative to the varieties grown.

The *rugosas* are probably the most popular in this respect. Like all roses they are not evergreen, but their foliage is large and leathery and will persist for a long period. Most important of all they are almost disease free and the majority will produce a fantastic harvest of large globular hips. The two great values of the *rugosa* family are they do not require seasonal pruning and provide a great deterrent to predators (usually human) with their very thorny stems. Planted about 60–90 cm (2–3 ft) apart, they provide an impenetrable barrier.

They do not take kindly to any form of cutting back – such treatment will produce ugly growth. They are far better allowed to grow naturally and cut back every five or six years to within 30 cm (1 ft) in the winter. Their natural resilience will produce a refurbished plant by the end of the next season. Not every garden requires a hedge as large as the rugosas and many shrub roses can

also produce good results. The Hybrid Musks, for example, are eminently satisfactory. For the smaller gardens many Floribundas will give great pleasure, but care must be taken to select bushy forms which will produce a nice rounded appearance; a line of bare stems is not a pretty sight.

Some of the prettiest effects can be obtained by the more vigorous patio roses, planted about 45 cm (1½ ft) apart. These create a fantastic strip of colour, which can provide quite a novel feature.

Finally, for the very big garden or estate, a hedge of some of the more robust ramblers is a memorable sight. Planted every 1.2 m (4 ft), they will require some support for the first two or three years but will quickly become established as a striking feature. This type of hedge is of course impossible to maintain, but in such a position would not require it. However, if constraint is required, the modern hedge trimmers will cope.

FORMAL BEDS

Since the introduction of the familiar modern bush rose, we have got used to the rose as a form of bedding plant. Indeed 'the rose garden' was and still is an ideal to which many gardeners aspire. The blaze of colour from early summer to late autumn gives immense pleasure and satisfaction.

· HEDGES ·

Many roses are ideal to add colour to the garden, making the most spectacular hedges. Planted about 90 cm (3 ft) apart, these varieties require little maintenance.

Name	Colour
Hybrid rugosa	
'Blanc Double de Coubert'	White
'Fru Dagmar Hastrup'	Light pink
Rosa rugosa 'Alba'	White
Rosa rugosa rubra	Claret
'Roseraie de l'Hay'	Wine-red
'Sarah van Fleet'	Pink
'Scabrosa'	Mauve-red
'Schneezwerg'	White
Hybrid musk	
'Buff Beauty'	Light apricot
'Cornelia'	Strawberry
'Felicia'	Light pink
'Moonlight'	Pale primrose
'Prosperity'	Creamy white
'Trier'	White
Floribunda	
'Iceberg'	White
'Mountbatten'	Yellow
The Queen Elizabeth Rose	Pink

'The Garland' is equally at
home clambering over
fences or growing through
trees and is a mass of flower
in mid-summer.

The majority of rose beds are situated in lawns, though modern design is demanding a more formal gravel backdrop with edges of stone or brick.

The choice of varieties is wide, and opinion varies on the greater merits of Floribundas or Hybrid teas. Of more concern is the planning or structuring of these beds, particularly as pruning is an annual maintenance task. Care must be taken not to plan a rose bed that is too wide. This will lead into difficulties of cultivation, with the risk of damage to precious plants as well as weeds caused by the gardener wielding implements. Equally, greater control can be obtained with spraying equipment.

The biggest debate is usually on the choice of variety or varieties. There is no doubt that the greatest and most stunning effect is created by planting beds of roses of a single variety; certainly a small bed will look a hotchpotch if too many varieties are used. In the latter situation, try using two varieties planted alternatively to give a pleasant blended effect.

For a long bed, size itself does have a dramatic quality but can lead to a dull uniformity of shape. The remedy is to introduce a different height, and plant standards or pillar roses of a compatible colour to your bush roses, to give variation.

Whatever size the garden, never plant rose bushes too close to an edge that has to be maintained. A distance of about 45 cm (1½ ft) may look generous, but not when the plants have become established. Trimming lawn edges with overhanging rose plants is a painful experience both to the trimmer and the rose!

▶ **Miniature and patio roses will add interest to the smallest gardens and enhance terraces and split-level planting schemes.**

Rock gardens

Statistically more roses die planted in rock gardens than any other plant in the garden. The reason is very simple: they are treated as alpines in this position and not allowed the root run or maintenance that a rose normally expects. Miniatures are most inappropriate in this position. Fortunately the introduction of some of the modern small ground coverers can contribute and will give great pleasure. 'Nozomi' and 'Snow Carpet' are two prime examples of the plant breeder's art, providing a valuable contribution from the genus *Rosa* to the rock garden. However, they must be planted in a pocket of fertile soil.

Herbaceous borders

To the purist, roses should only be grown in solitary splendour, without competition from other plants. But fashion has changed and most gardeners recognize the tremendous contribution roses can make to a mixed herbaceous border, if they are planted wisely and the correct variety is chosen. The greatest mistake that is made is to ignore the fact that the rose, probably more than any other garden plant, requires the maximum amount of sunlight, particularly early in the year. The great contribution that the rose can make to an herbaceous border, therefore, is for suitable varieties like the bigger Floribundas and shrub roses to be planted in groups of three, five or seven in positions relative to their height, and prevent competition from heavy broad-leaved spring plants that will cut out the light. Solitary-planted bush roses are a great disappointment and are usually lost in the 'jungle'.

A valuable contribution to colour can also be obtained by using the rose when not in flower as a foliage plant. The specie *Rosa glauca (Rosa rubrifolia)* is probably the most dramatic with its purplish foliage. *Rosa moyesii* 'Geranium' will provide fantastic colour in the autumn with its harvest of bright red hips. The Floribunda, The Times Rose, with its deep green, almost purple foliage, is quite stunning and is a rightful successor to 'Europeana', now sadly discounted with its tendency to mildew.

Raised beds

Low hollow walls and raised beds demand special treatment. They are an important part of the garden which can go horribly wrong. Assumed to be the natural home for 'rock plants', this type of plant can only contribute for a short period in the spring. Patio roses, miniatures and modern ground covers will give colour for a greater length

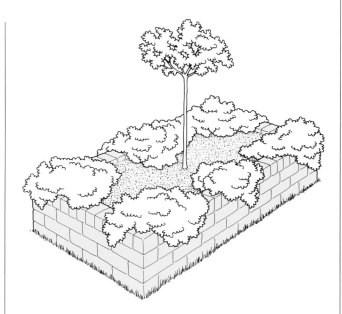

Fig. 5 **Raised bed with ground cover roses and a half-standard to give added height.**

of time (Fig. 5). It is important that the soil to make up these situations is both plentiful and of a good quality. The addition of water-holding organic matter will help, but frequent heavy watering is essential in prolonged periods of drought. In such restricted positions, frequent refurbishment of the top 8–10 cm (3–4 in) of soil is a great help; about every two years will keep them happy.

Specimen shrubs

It is common practice these days to devote an area of the garden to conservation. Although a meadow with wild flowers is a perfect delight, there comes a time when something more exciting is wanted, particularly in early summer. Some varieties of rose will give unexpected colour and some of the bigger shrubs are ideal for this part of the garden.

The secret of a well-grown specimen rose plant is to give it a good start, and protection from predators until it has become established. You can do this by planting it inside a cage and encouraging new growth with a form of support to see it through its juvenile stage (Fig. 6). Many plants have to combat grass growing right up to the plant. This is a mistake. The soil immediately below the rose must be kept clear of all weed, and mulched annually with compost and the occasional boost of a good rose fertilizer. Specimen bushes in this part of the garden must be selected with little demand on maintenance.

Containers

Growing roses in pots is an art that was perfected by gardeners some 100 years ago, when standards and ramblers were grown to provide mobile splashes of colour at various functions. Sadly economic factors discouraged this practice and only recently has this method become popular again. This is as much a reflection of the material

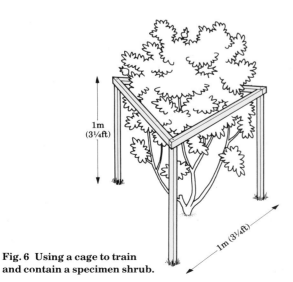

Fig. 6 Using a cage to train and contain a specimen shrub.

1m (3¼ft)

1m (3¼ft)

available as custom. A considerable proportion of rose plants now sold are containerized as a method of distribution, but this must not be confused with growing roses in a pot, patio or tub. Primarily the rose has a large root system and this fact has to be acknowledged when choosing the right receptacle. Secondly, notwithstanding the advance of plastic, the majority of plants will grow far more satisfactorily in wooden tubs or stone or clay pottery. Good drainage is the primary concern, but the volume of available soil is of equal importance; a container with less than a cubic foot of soil is a trial to the plant. Varieties are much the choice of the gardener but avoid the ordinary Hybrid teas and Floribundas and go for the newer miniature climbers, patios and the more vigorous but recurrent-flowering ground covers.

Use a good quality potting soil (compost) with a high proportion of peat (or peat substitute). This will ensure a certain degree of protection against drying out. Nevertheless, any plant in a container must be fed and watered regularly, and repotted once a year.

PROBLEM AREAS

No garden is perfect, and every gardener has a problem area. Sometimes this is a bed, but more commonly it is a particular position where nothing appears to grow. Solving these irritants can be a costly exercise unless one is aware of the occasional basic rule that will smooth the course and make life much simpler.

● *Dry soil* In temperate zones garden plants are dependent on a moderate rainfall. The rose is no different but does have the advantage of possessing a root system that can reach to extraordinary depths. Irrigation is not mandatory but rather a help to get a plant established. Indeed, to make a rose dependent on artificial irrigation can do much harm as the roots will not look for water. However it is important that newly planted trees in a dry spring get some help. Container grown roses must be watered if planted in late spring or early summer. Some newly planted climbing and rambling roses appear to be reluctant to start into growth. One or two heavy soakings – at least three or four buckets of water per plant – will remedy this situation.

● *Waterlogged soil* can be very detrimental to many plants and is usually caused by bad drainage. This can be controlled by either raising the level of the rose beds or digging land drains to dispose of surplus water. Occasionally gardens can become flooded in winter storms but, provided the water can drain away quickly, there should be no lasting damage.

● *Heavy clay soils* can become difficult and unmanageable in the winter months, and damage can be caused to the structure if handled in this state. The remedy here is two-fold. Firstly, complete any cultivation by early autumn and allow the frost to break up the soil in the winter months to produce a friable tilth in the spring. In addition, the application of copious dressings of coarse sand and organic waste will open up the soil, aid cultivation and encourage a sound root system.

● *Shade* can be another problem. At the risk of repetition, a rose does react strongly to the amount of light it receives, and indeed there are few plants that do not. Roses simply will not grow in heavy shade underneath broad-leaved trees, but there are several varieties (particularly climbers and ramblers) that appear to thrive on north or north-east walls. However, even here they

'Pheasant' (pink) and 'Grouse' (pale pink) are typical of the modern type of vigorous ground cover that will grow in many difficult areas in the garden.

must receive a modicum of light, as in an open courtyard with reflected light or positions of a similar nature. Although these varieties appear to thrive in such positions, do not expect the flower content to be high. Dappled light is quite acceptable and many of the new ground covers are quite happy in this situation. The impossible situation is the north or sunless border of a beech hedge or a similar shallow-rooted plant, where it is likely to be very dry, without light and probably a poor soil.

Many gardens are limited to the amount of light they receive but are still able to grow a few roses. The modern patio types appear to withstand these conditions, as also can many of the shorter-growing Hybrid teas and Floribundas. To grow the normally very vigorous types will only produce an ugly and stressed plant. On walls and fences, try to grow the recurrent-flowering climbers rather than the older varieties which will only produce copious amounts of foliage.

● *Draughts and winds* are two of the commonest causes of plant damage, and there is not a garden in the town or country that has not fallen victim at some time in its history. The remedy is very simple, although some situations can produce special problems. It is not generally realized that a rose in its early months of existence is subject to all the vagaries of inclement weather. Young rose plants are produced in big open fields where they are subject to every imaginable weather condition. In gardens, conditions can be aggravated by the position of buildings, hedges or woodland. In effect this means that draughts can be induced which can have very damaging results. An 'advantageous' gap in a hedge, or a badly designed building complex, can do irreparable harm and it is unfair to expect a plant to thrive under those conditions.

'Simba', one of the shorter Hybrid teas that justifies the description 'the perfect bedding rose'. It will produce a succession of flowers throughout the summer.

Wind is a totally different impediment, which most plants will cope with provided they are cared for. In practice this means that vigorous young shoots on climbers and ramblers must be carefully tied in as they grow. (The use of soft string is recommended.) Standards must be well secured and inspected at regular intervals to check for faulty ties and dubious stakes.

Commonsense will tell you not to grow standards in very windy situations, but the rose is a tough plant and will succeed in the most difficult situations.

· 3 ·
<u>Planning and Purchasing</u>

More often than not the new owner of a garden has very fixed ideas about how it should look and it is human nature to want to demolish everything in sight and start afresh. This is a great mistake and patience is the order of the day. If time is on the gardener's side, by all means tidy up the garden but give time, in fortunate circumstances a whole season of flowering, to discover the plants that already exist. Some astonishing instances have occurred where weeds have been removed to reveal the most acceptable plants. Old and derelict gardens can reveal the most intriguing plants which could well have been cleared in a fit of exuberance. In the matter of roses, neglected subjects have a remarkable history of being revitalized after a good heavy trim.

Know your soil
In temperate climates there are very few areas where it is impossible to grow roses. However, the indigenous soil can have a vast influence on the type and range of varieties. There is an old adage that roses will only grow on heavy clay soils; this may have been true years ago but with better understanding of soil management, this fallacy is somewhat dated.

The simple reason for the superiority of heavy soils was a dependence on organic feeds. Farmyard manure was in great abundance and the very nature of soil control was the dependence on a limitless supply of this natural commodity. The structure of clays was a gift to the organic regime. The ideal soil is a heavy loam – a mixture of clay and sand with a good proportion on silt.

Because today gardens are sited in the most inappropriate places, we must become more adaptable. Very light soils can be strengthened with the addition of inert composts such as peat or a peat substitute. However, they will always remain 'hungry' – that is, they will always absorb fertilizers at a greater speed than the clays.

Chalky soils will never grow roses successfully so one should only grow plants recommended for this medium or, if roses are particularly desired, investigate the various ways of growing them in containers or raised beds with imported soil.

A well-drained soil is very important. Great problems can be caused by landscaping. This means that areas of made-up soil will appear waterlogged until such time that the soil structure finds a natural drainage. Do not be persuaded to construct expensive drainage schemes until the soil has time to settle.

Planting distances
All planning must be devised with both aesthetic and practical considerations. There is, however, room for personal likes and dislikes.

When planning a large bed, space must be given to cultivate the plants without damaging

· HANDY TIP ·

Before ordering plants, mark out very carefully and accurately the positions in the garden where you propose to site them. Leaving a rose order short can result in expensive additional carriage costs and possible disappointment if varieties are sold out.

them. In an ideal world the perfect bed of roses should be four or five plants deep, that is approximately 3 m (9 ft) or 3.5 m (11 ft) wide. This will enable weed control and spraying to be completed comfortably.

● *The average bush rose* should be planted 60 cm (2 ft) apart from its neighbour, and if the surrounding area is grass then a distance of 45 cm (1½ ft) must be allowed from the edge of the bed to the first plant (Fig. 7). The length of the bed is less important, but anything too long encourages visitors to cut through and damage plants.

Small beds should adhere to these measurements. To reduce planting distances will cause severe overcrowding and increase the incidence of disease, and widths much in excess will look ugly and encourage weeds.

● *Standards* can look ugly and regimented if they are planted too close together and a distance of 2–2.5 m (6–8 ft) is to be recommended. There is a tendency to allow a standard too much space at ground level in a rose bed, thereby creating thin plantings. Plant rose bushes fairly closely up to a standard.

● *Climbers* will look dreadfully overcrowded if planted too close together. Although 3 m (10 ft) would appear to be too wide, given their natural growth they will quickly produce a tapestry of

colour. Never plant climbers too close to doorways or paths, and keep well away from the base of walls (about 45 cm or 1½ ft).

Catalogue descriptions

Height and vigour is a subject that compilers of rose catalogues are justifiably hesitant in quoting, and the astute composer of these sometimes graphic descriptions will rarely give an objective opinion. Most measurements are given in a comparative way. To describe a plant as 'bushy' usually infers that it is rounded but robust, as compared to, say, 'vigorous and tall', which means just that. In a moderate temperature climate a good bedding bush rose is expected to grow to maturity at about 1 m (3 ft) if it is pruned conventionally. A 'vigorous' bush will grow anywhere between 1.2–2 m (4–6½ ft) tall. If a rambler is described as vigorous, then expect it to be capable of making 3 m (10 ft) of growth in a season. A climber that is described as a good

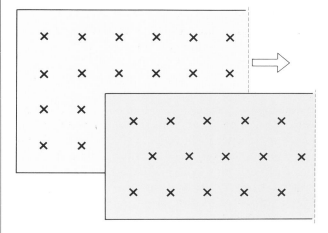

Fig. 7 **Alternative methods of measuring and marking out a formal bed of rose bushes. In both plans the basic principle of 60cm (2ft) tree to tree and 45cm (18in) distance from edge of bed has been adhered to.**

27

'Iceberg' and The Times Rose, two popular Floribundas famous for their abundance of flower and continuity.

subject for a pillar will be 3 m (10 ft) when mature. Standards are quite specifically advertised at the height they are propagated.

Mode of despatch

New rose plants all begin life at a rose nursery. Their method of despatch, offer for sale and the season of the year will determine the mode that the purchaser will eventually receive them.

● *Bare-root plants* are the norm if the plant is purchased direct from the nursery or through mail order. It is normally lifted in early autumn, graded, labelled and stored prior to despatch. This type of plant will give the best results if received and planted before it turns cold, but can also be quite successful when planted in early spring.

● *Root wraps* are bare-root plants that have been packed in a sleeve, usually with an illustration of the variety and some moisture-retaining material wrapped around the roots. This is the type of plant obtainable from hardware stores and other retail outlets. As it is normally packaged very early in the season it must be handled with care. Retailers do not always store these plants properly and they can sometimes become rather dry. Once purchased, treat as bare-root plants.

• *Containerized roses* are bare-root plants that have been potted during the winter, pruned at the conventional time in the spring and grown on to become available from the end of the bare-root season. The rose is not an easy plant to containerize and must be watered daily until planted, especially in dry weather. They give best results if planted before mid-summer.

When to plant
The householder new to gardening is often confused by the plethora of advice which is given in the gardening columns of the press, television programmes or the wise sages at his club. One of the most confusing is the correct time to plant.

• *Autumn planting* Given an ideal friable loam which has been well prepared, there is no doubt that planting in late autumn is probably the most successful using bare-root plants – always provided, of course, that the nurseries have commenced lifting. And this is the problem. To lift, grade and despatch in the matter of a few weeks is a monumental exercise and tries even the most efficient organizations.

• *Spring planting* can also be successful with bare-root plants if care is taken to keep the roots moist. Probably the best advice to give in these circumstances is to prune plants, particularly bushes, before planting. This has two advantages. It not only saves the back muscles, but avoids stress on the plants which do not have to maintain extraneous growth, whilst at the same time endeavouring to produce a viable root system. However, spring planting is only really successful in gardens where irrigation is available to cope with spring droughts.

• *All-year planting.* The greatest difficulty is contending with conditions in heavy wet clay soils. This has now been ameliorated with widespread acceptance of containerized rose plants. This has enabled the planting season to be extended and very good results have been obtained in the most difficult situations. A further advantage can be gained using this type of plant to replace trees that have not survived the winter.

'Matangi' is probably the most successful of the 'hand-painted' roses and is also very useful as a cut flower variety with a long vase life.

No matter which method of planting is adopted, it must be borne in mind that as the season progresses the choice of varieties is inevitably somewhat restricted. For the purist who demands a particular variety, early ordering is absolutely essential. Do not expect the same wide range in containers at your local garden centre as are on offer in a comprehensive catalogue.

There is no such thing in gardening as a cheap plant. Many offers are made extolling the virtues of a particular package and it is fair comment that the majority have considerable merit; but avoid lost-label collections and similar offers.

Also plants that are readily available in supermarkets and garage forecourts very early in the autumn are at a high risk. It takes some time from lifting to grading, packaging and despatching to some of the distribution points, which means in effect that they must have been lifted far too early in the late summer, before they have had the opportunity to be properly ripened. A point worth remembering is that no matter where the plant is sold, if the conditions are not good for storage the plant cannot be expected to give results when planted. Overheated stores, plants exposed to full sunlight, garage forecourts with no experienced care, is anathema to young plants.

Looking for a healthy plant

There are minimum standards generally accepted by the rose trade for quality plants (Fig. 8). There is a British Standard and an EC regulation which is usually demanded by public bodies and local authorities. The measurements expected in those instances are a minimum and a high-quality plant is well above these criteria.

● *A good fibrous root system* should be apparent on a bare-root plant, with a minimum length of 25 cm (10 in) from the collar (that is the point that it is propagated at) to the root tip. The roots must never have been allowed to dry out and the plant should be delivered in a moist condition.

● *The top growth* can vary according to the variety. It is the norm that a bush rose can be trimmed but there must be a minimum of 30 cm (1 ft) in length. Shrubs and climbers must have a minimum of 45 cm (18 in). The tops must be neatly cut and no torn branches must be apparent. Opinion varies on the size and number of shoots but most suppliers would agree that three constitutes a high-quality plant, with each the circumference of a small finger. However, if the

---

· BUYING FOR QUALITY ·

Bare-root
● The stems should be at least 30 cm (12 in) long.
● Grade one plants must have two stems with a circumference the size of a pencil. (These are minimum sizes, most plants are bigger with three stems.)
● The stems must look fresh and not shrivelled.
● The roots must be at least 25 cm (10 in) long. They must be fibrous and in a moist condition.
● If they are root wrapped the holding material must be damp, the stems of the same minimum size as the bare root and there should be no sign of them growing out. The plant should not be showing any leaves.

Containerized rose plants
● The top growth should match the quality shown on a bare-root plant (see above).
● Purchased after early spring they must be properly pruned relative to the variety and any subsequent growth should be free of disease.
● The compost they are planted in must be well watered but not waterlogged.
● A few weeds on the surface of the compost in the container are acceptable. However, avoid containers that are so full of weeds that they're spreading and seeding everywhere. This would indicate a degree of neglect in the nursery, results of which may become apparent much later.

· HANDY TIP ·

If a rose order is placed with a nursery late in the season there is a very good chance that some of the varieties will be sold out. It is therefore advisable to save time and lengthy correspondence by naming substitutes. Alternatively, state on the order form quite clearly that any shortfall can be made up by the nursery.

branches are substantially bigger, two stems are adequate and indeed some varieties will only produce that number.

The overall size of patios and miniatures and some of the smaller ground covers is correspondingly smaller. Standard roses are considered good quality possessing at least two arms each, with two shoots and the stem of robust stature.

Where to view roses

● *Mail-order catalogues* Choosing the correct variety is a personal choice and there are many ways of doing this. A *bona-fide* rose grower will produce a colour catalogue which can be a great help. If they are also breeders, or agents for breeders, their particular varieties will have a high priority. Catalogues make very interesting reading and can help, but remember that the colour printing is not always accurate.

● *Exhibitions and flower shows* are both exciting to attend and will give the potential customer considerable guidance. Remember that plants shown early in the season have probably been forced under glass, so the colours will be purer and the size of the bloom much bigger, and of course the visitor is only able to see those varieties which show well.

● *Gardens* are probably the main source of information and obviously the choice is much wider. In the UK The Royal National Rose Society and The Royal Horticultural Society have big gardens where a massive range of varieties can be seen. There is a list at the end of this book giving a wide range of big gardens that can be visited in many countries.

The greatest help that can be given to the bewildered budding horticulturist is to visit local gardens. There is ample opportunity to do this, with many benevolent schemes an added incentive. Not only does this provide you with a chance to speak to the gardeners concerned; probably of greater importance, it is possible to see the range of varieties that flourish in your particular locality.

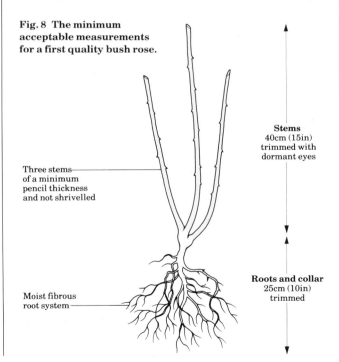

Fig. 8 The minimum acceptable measurements for a first quality bush rose.

Three stems of a minimum pencil thickness and not shrivelled

Moist fibrous root system

Stems 40cm (15in) trimmed with dormant eyes

Roots and collar 25cm (10in) trimmed

● *Rose nurseries* are also mostly open to inspection and are pleased to receive visitors. Their fields are well labelled and there is the opportunity to wander round the roses and ponder for hours, without any pressure to buy, and enjoy the countryside. Because rose fields grow what we call maiden plants, they will not be in full flower until some time after the similar varieties in established gardens – probably about two or three weeks later. Some of these nurseries also have established gardens where the mature product can be inspected.

Labels
Every new rose plant must be labelled, whether it is received from a nursery or garden centre. The information differs widely but generally there must be a name, usually the type, and sometimes the colour. On the reverse is the name of the supplier, which need not necessarily be the grower. Some nurseries indicate that it is the subject of a plant copyright (patent), which infers that you are not allowed to propagate it for sale without a licence. The most important information is the name. The type can be misleading. Never buy unlabelled or 'lost-label collections'.

Ordering
Because a rose plant has to be propagated some time ahead of the date it is offered for sale (usually about eighteen months), there is an inevitable gamble by the rose nurseries to forecast accurately the numbers that will be in demand for each variety. As the selling season progresses, some varieties will be in greater demand than others and 'sold out' lists appear. The moral of this story is that if you have any

◀ Rose fields are at their peak of perfection in mid-summer. Plants are usually well labelled and can give great pleasure to visitors.

special selections in mind, order early – by that I mean late summer, as 'sold out' lists begin to appear from early autumn.

COMPANION PLANTS

The concept of growing plants other than roses would have been anathema to the purist rose buff until relatively recently. The purist would demand that there was no place in the rose bed for any other plant and indeed would expect to be ostracized for condoning such licence. With the increase in land values and the subsequent diminishing of gardens, however, there is a

'Nozomi' (bottom right), 'Red Max Graf' (centre) and 'Bonica' are contrasting styles of modern ground covers which have become so popular in gardens today.

33

· ROSE PETAL WINE ·

The scent of roses has a lingering quality which can be captured and retained in many ways. The most popular form is to make rose-petal wine. The recipe and method are very simple.

Ingredients

2 litres (4 pt) rose petals	*1.5 kilos (3 lb) sugar*
4.5 litres (1 gal) boiling	*1 Campden tablet*
water	*1 lemon*
500 g (18 oz) sultanas	*Wine yeast*

In mid-summer on a hot dry day gather rose petals. Place them in a bucket of boiling water and stand for two days stirring occasionally. Strain off the essence and pour in a demi-john, adding sultanas and sugar. Sterilize with a Campden tablet for 24 hours and then add a wine yeast. Fit with an airlock and ferment to a finish. Rack off, add a Campden tablet and bottle.

This will mature with age but makes the basis of a good spritzer drunk cool with a slice of lemon. The best wines are made from red petals from a single variety.

· ROSE HIP 'SHERRY' ·

In the autumn the hedgerows are full of nature's harvest. Rose hips, the fruit of the dog rose (*R. canina*), product of a bountiful summer, can be gathered to make a very acceptable country wine.

Ingredients

2 kilos (4 lb) rose hips	*Sherry yeast*
1.5 kilos (3 lb) sugar	*1 Campden tablet*
1 lemon	*Brandy (optional)*
4.5 litres (1 gal) boiling	
water	

For every 2 kilos (4 lbs) of hips you will require 1½ kilos (3 lbs) of sugar and one lemon. Mince the rose hips, picked after a good frost, place in a bucket with the juice of a lemon and boiling water. When cool add sherry yeast, cover, and allow to ferment for two weeks. Strain into a demi-john and close with an air-lock. Ferment to a finish, filter, add one Campden tablet and bottle. This will mature in about twelve months.

The addition of a modest drop of brandy will produce a libation guaranteed to ease any self inflicted pain when pruning.

tremendous competition for every plant and roses have to take their turn.

In truth, it can be argued that with the widespread use of weedkillers, particularly in rose beds, there is little incentive to introduce other plants. Nevertheless even the keenest rosarian would accept that for a good part of the winter and early spring a rose bed is not the most exciting part of the garden and there is certainly room to give colour to these areas during those dreary months.

Priority must be given to the roses, allowing access to pruning, spraying and the application of fertilizers, weed deterrents and mulches. In addition, as mentioned in Chapter 2, the rose is very dependent on the amount of light it receives, particularly during spring.

Plants that will impede proper cultivation

There is a compulsive attitude among some gardeners to produce swathes of crude colour, particularly early in the year. The tulip is to the forefront of this type of plant and its use in rose beds is an invitation to disaster as the broad leaves cut out the light at the most critical time of year. Many rose beds have simply faded away, unable to get a good start in the spring. The other plant that can cause complications is the small creeping type, which introduced to a rose bed can become invasive and physically prevent the natural cultivation of the rose.

Giving early colour to a rose bed

The most natural plant to give colour in early spring is the daffodil. The narrow leaves and early maturity do not interfere with the roses' struggle for light. Planted in small groups well away from the base of the rose plants, especially in new beds, they can give great pleasure. Groups of dwarf iris may also be used to advantage.

● *Formal beds* are the most difficult but can be enhanced with edges of the dwarf lavender *Lavendula* var. 'Munstead' or the ubiquitous box *Buxus sempervirens* 'Suffructicosa'. Using either of these plants, mention must be made of the fact that they are host to an incredible number of predators who regard them as a home from home in the winter months. Care should therefore be taken to spray them with the same thoroughness, at the same time as dealing with your roses.

● *Mixed borders* where roses predominate can be brightened with shrubs that will lend colour in the dullest season of the year. Some of the evergreen berberis will break a dull border. Most of the mahonias give colour in the spring in darker areas of the garden. The shrubs that will give colour for the longest periods are the *Elaeagnus* varieties. *Elaeagnus pungens* 'Maculata', with its yellow and green leaves, must have pride of place and is also a refreshing addition to flower arrangements to minimize the rather dull evergreens during the coldest months. Other members of this family to warrant consideration are *Elaeagnus × ebbingei* 'Gilt Edge', green leaves margined with gold, and *Elaeagnus augustifolia* 'Oleaster', with silvery grey leaves. There are of course a bewildering list of herbaceous perennial plants but the accent must be to provide colour when it is at a premium in the garden.

● *For large rose shrubs and climbing roses*, clematis is the perfect companion plant, but they are also the plant which will cause the biggest problems. The very nature of clematis means that they excel growing on other vegetative material in preference to artifically manufactured pergolas and wire. The rose is a natural support and here comes the rub: over-enthusiastic gardeners will plant clematis before the selected rose has been allowed to establish itself. The rule therefore is to restrain enthusiasm and allow climbers and ramblers to become well settled before being asked to provide support. The choice of varieties is numerous but it is wise to select those that flower late and require to be pruned at much the same time as the host plant. The faster-growing and more robust varieties of climbers and ramblers are the most suitable. The white 'Mme Alfred Carrière', the lovely 'Mermaid' or the fast-growing 'Cécile Brunner' are fabulous when festooned with an appropriate clematis.

Clematis varieties to be recommended are the *jackmanii* types, and of these the best are:

Name	Colour
Ascotiensis	Bright blue
Comtesse de Bouchaud	Mauve pink
Gipsy Queen	Violet-purple
Hagley Hybrid	Dark rosy-mauve
Jackmanii Superba	Rich velvety purple
Mme Baron Veillard	Lilac rose
Madame Edouard André	Dusky red
Perle d'Azure	Sky blue
Star of India	Deep purple blue
Victoria	Rose purple

One final word on plant associations. There was a popular belief that honeysuckles were not accepted in a rose garden as they were deemed to be hostages to aphids. Either greenfly have changed their eating habits or we are growing different varieties.

· 4 ·
Preparation and Planting

Planting a rose tree is a task that can be done at virtually any time of the year simply because of the various modes that have become available recently. However the factor determining this operation, like so much in the garden, is controlled by the weather.

When to plant
Provided the soil has been prepared, late-autumn would appear to be the most rewarding time and will give the best results. The advantage in planting at this time is two-fold. Far better to plant before the winter sets in; and of greater importance, the soil will still be warm enough to encourage good root growth, an advantage which is handsomely obvious when the plants are enabled to obtain an early start in the spring. Circumstances might preclude against completing autumn planting and of necessity the gardener will have to take advantage of mild dry days throughout the winter.

Bare-root planting must be finished by early spring; a dry warm period after that time can cause much damage and will necessitate heavy watering. Conversely, great damage can be done to the soil structure if it is on the heavy side and waterlogged during preparation.

● *Container-grown roses* are obviously planted from late spring onwards, when they become available in garden centres, and *must* be watered in. There is little advantage to be gained by planting containerized roses after mid-summer. They will be under great stress to produce autumn flower and plants purchased at this time are rarely of first quality and are usually very expensive.

Tools
There are many modern aids to gardening which will contribute to the well-being of the plants, but the basic range of tools has not altered much over the years.

● *A spade* is an obvious necessity and must be chosen with care. A well-sprung wooden-handled implement must be selected, which the operator will find comfortable to use. There are many fancy looking implements with lots of chrome plating, but a well-tempered blade which can be kept sharp and clean is the criterion.

● *A well-sprung fork* also needs to be chosen for ease of use.

● *A spring rake* is not high on the list but is useful for clearing up.

● *A hoe* may appear to be a primitive tool in the garden but it is essential. There is a temptation to dig over an established rose bed in early spring which is the worst thing you can do. The plants

'Sweet Magic' is a perfect example of the true patio rose with miniaturized flowers and foliage.

will be loosened, the fibrous root system damaged and the whole exercise is futile, although cosmetically it may look pretty. A good hoeing is of greater benefit.

● *A heavy thump hammer* will be required to drive in standard stakes, together with a good supply of straight-grained stakes and tree ties.

Much is made of hiring small mechanical machines for the production of a good tilth; however unless the soil is on the dry side and very friable, they will cause more harm than good and have been known to destroy the structure of the soil and put back the cultivation of the garden by as much as a season.

PREPARING THE GROUND

Probably the one operation which cannot be neglected when planting roses is the cultivation of the site and its soil. There is no short cut to preparing a good rose bed. Although essentially the operation is simply digging the soil over and incorporating a good organic compost from a reputable source, there is much more to the exercise than that. The soil must be cleared of all perennial weed roots. This may require forking before the spade is used. Digging itself is quite an art but extraordinarily satisfying.

Digging

Many soils have a good depth of fertility but others may be damaged if the lower spit is brought to the surface. This is more relevant in chalky/ limestone regions and some sandy gardens.

Soils that have been in cultivation for some time have a tendency to obtain a 'hard pan'. That is a curious barrier of almost cement-like structure some 30–45 cm (1–1½ ft) below ground level. It is wise, therefore, to give time to deep cultivation or double digging the prospective rose bed, making sure the bottom spit is moved, loosened, but not brought to the surface (Fig. 9). As the digging proceeds, manure should be integrated to raise the fertility.

Fig. 9 Double digging should be done well ahead of marking out and planting to allow soil to settle.

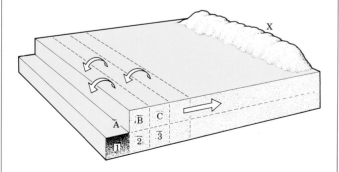

1. Remove a spit of soil (A) to position X.
2. Subsoil 1 is broken up with fork, integrating good farmyard manure or garden compost.
3. Next spit of soil (B) is dug over to position A, working in sand or peat if required.
4. Subsoil 2 is forked and so on.

In some heavier soils the addition of sand and or peat (or peat substitute) will open up the structure and encourage an improved root system. On light sandy soils there is no real substitute for well-prepared manure or garden compost.

In an ideal world this should all be completed before the plants arrive, which all seems onerous and time consuming, but if a rose plant is expected to give satisfaction for a number of years this time is not wasted. The soil can sometimes be too acid, usually indicated by rhododendrons growing well. An indication of this can be obtained by using a 'pH kit' available from garden shops. The ideal reading for roses is 6.5. Should the reading be below this a handful of ground limestone per sq metre (sq yard) applied well before planting will help.

Manuring

All plants in the garden respond handsomely when planted in a fertile soil, which means in effect ensuring that there is an abundance of good quality organic manure available. This is obviously a commodity which is more readily accessible in rural areas. Even with an abundance it is well to establish that the manure has been well stacked for a minimum period of six months; fresh farmyard manure is lethal. Alternatively, there are many methods of producing home-made garden compost using the detritus of old plants, vegetable waste and kitchen refuse. Care must be taken to break it down well and there are many additives to achieve this. Be careful never to use lawn cuttings where weed-killers have been used. Failing all this, there is no lack of products in garden centres, but first satisfy yourself that they have enough food value and are appropriate therefore for the job in hand. There is some credence in the theory that compost made from a garden lacking in vital constituents,

· PLANTING TIME FOR ROSES ·

Bare-root plants	Early autumn to early spring; late pruning in the spring is not recommended but, if this is necessary, prune bush roses before planting and water in.
Root-wrapped plants	These are, in reality, bare-root plants that have received some form of protection to prevent them drying out. Immediately on receipt, unpack and soak in water for a good hour before planting. They are normally available at the same time as bare-root plants.
Containerized plants	The concept of container-grown roses is to make them available when the bare-root season has finished. In fact they can be planted at any time of the year but it is advantageous to use them in the late spring or early summer. They are expensive in comparison to bare root and there is little advantage in planting after mid-summer as they require constant watering.

for example lime, will perpetuate this frailty. If this should be so, correct immediately with a dressing.

Planting mixtures

The young rose tree, whether it has been lifted from the nursery or knocked out of a container, has received a considerable shock when moved. The fabric of the tree has probably been cut back quite hard and the root system has certainly been curtailed significantly. The young maiden rose plant which you are expecting to thrive in your garden should have been lifted at the proper season, is a very tough subject and difficult to kill; it has nevertheless undergone a traumatic experience and must be re-located with every possible consideration. This is where the use of a planting mixture is an absolute necessity.

A planting mixture is literally a medium or environment which surrounds the roots of a young plant to provide them with an added incentive to become established as quickly and as successfully as possible. It provides a medium for the young roots to grow into before venturing into the coarse indigenous soil, whether it be an inhospitable clay or a hungry sand.

Planting mixtures consist of a preparation of a friable material – usually peat or a peat substitute – and bonemeal, roughly in the proportion of a handful of bonemeal to a bucket of peat. Other mixtures contain well-prepared leafmould and light loamy soil. Manure should not be added to this unless it is *very* well rotted.

Marking out

The secret of quick and efficient planting is thorough preparation, and marking out is quite the most important task. Although a rough

Fig. 10 Planting sequence.

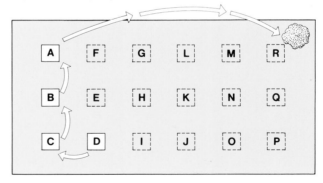

1. Mark out bed (see Fig. 7 on page 27).
2. Dig hole at A and place soil near final planting.
3. Place plant in position A against marker (see Fig. 11 on page 42).
4. Dig hole at B, planting first rose at A together with soil from B.
5. Position plant B and plant with soil from C.
6. Continue until final position, when soil from position A is utilized.

◄'Bantry Bay' is a very good example of the modern climber which will flower for a very long period in the summer and autumn.

► 'Paul Sherville', a lovely salmon pink Hybrid tea, has all the attributes which make for a good standard, bushy growth and handsome foliage.

calculation would have been made before ordering, a precise measurement with rod and line is vital and will simplify the procedure. Use a stick marked off every 60 cm (2 ft) as a measuring rod (a broomstick is ideal). The outer dimensions of the bed can be shown with a washing line or length of string. Short canes about 45 cm (1½ ft) long are suitable for marking the position of the roses. Whatever the size of beds, the effect of good accurate planting is pleasing to the eye.

PLANTING

Care of plants on arrival

In the normal course of events the plants will arrive bare-rooted in the late autumn. They will require unpacking immediately, although modern methods of despatch usually ensure no deterioration if left unpacked for a few days.

Nevertheless circumstances may preclude immediate planting and they will have to be heeled in. If by chance the soil is frozen, do not unpack; store in a frost-free but cool storage area, and unpack as soon as possible, when conditions improve.

● *Heeling in* is simply digging a trench somewhere in the garden, unpacking the plants and laying them out so that the roots are well covered with soil temporarily until there is time to plant them properly. If the bundles are too big, cut the ties and spread the roots out. Big bundles have a nasty habit of drying out if this is not done. In open weather commence planting the moment they arrive. They just require dipping in a bucket of water (never plant dry roots) but do not soak.

Container plants will require watering regularly once a day until planted.

41

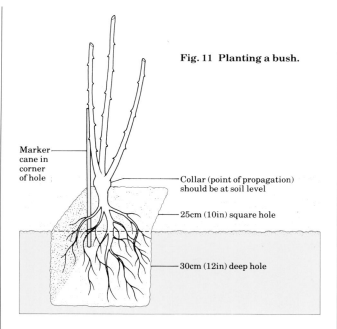

Fig. 11 Planting a bush.

Marker cane in corner of hole

Collar (point of propagation) should be at soil level

25cm (10in) square hole

30cm (12in) deep hole

Fig. 12 Planting a climber or rambler.

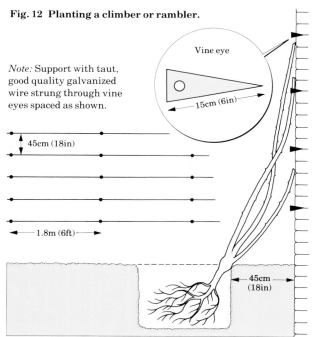

Note: Support with taut, good quality galvanized wire strung through vine eyes spaced as shown.

Vine eye

15cm (6in)

45cm (18in)

1.8m (6ft)

45cm (18in)

Planting a bare-root/root-wrapped bush (Fig. 11)

Provided the proper preparation of the soil and the marking out has been completed, the process of planting is simple. Dig a hole about 25 cm by 25 cm (10 in × 10 in) and 30 cm (12 in) deep, leaving the marker peg so situated that the final position of the marker is in the corner of the hole. The soil removed should be placed near the position of the final tree to be planted. The procedure is then to place the designated variety up against the marker, allowing the roots to spread out and to allow the soil level to be at the junction of the tree and the roots, which is normally at the position it was propagated. A good large handful of planting mixture is then added, encompassing the roots. The hole for the second tree is then prepared and this soil is then used to plant the first tree and so on and so on.

● *Treading* As the operation proceeds, care must be taken to tread in the plants thoroughly and firmly. Loose planting is disastrous and can lead to a high mortality rate, and would appear to encourage suckers. Planting roses, particularly large numbers, can be expedited quickly and effectively by this method. In a wet season circumstances may prevent treading properly, in which case this must be done at the earliest opportunity and repeated following a frosty winter in the spring before they are pruned.

Planting a climber/rambler (Fig. 12)

A new climber or rambler is planted by much the same method as is applied to a bush, with one big difference. Many plants of this type are planted on new sites, particularly where building has recently been completed. In this case, the position for a new plant against a wall or similar structure may have to be thoroughly prepared. This will necessitate removing about 3 cu ft (1½ ft × 1½ ft

× 1½ ft) of detritus, and making the position up with imported soil or compost – 1 part well-rotted compost or manure, 2 parts good garden soil and 1 part peat or a peat substitute. This mixture can be enhanced with a handful of good bonemeal per cu m (c yd). Plant climbers 45 cm (18 in) away from the wall.

Planting a standard (Fig. 13)

A standard rose is in some respects often viewed as a somewhat tedious and demanding plant in the garden. Neither a bush nor a tree, it tends to invite a considerable nuisance value in its positioning, and consequently suffers because of this. It is certainly the most expensive type of rose the gardener is ever likely to purchase and must be treated with due respect and forethought.

The position will have been marked out, bearing in mind the criteria and measurements discussed earlier in this book (see pages 21–23). However, it is well to repeat that it is prone to wind damage and will therefore obviously not be positioned in a very exposed position. All gardens are wind prone to some extent, but there is little point in inviting damage.

The majority of standards are propagated on a stem with a very fibrous root which is prone to drying out. Immediately on arrival in the garden, unpack the plant, dip it in water and heel in, thus protecting it from drying winds. Dip in water again immediately before planting and, of crucial importance, use plenty of planting mixture.

● *Staking* is a necessity and the stake must be positioned prior to planting. Good straight-grained wooden poles 5 cm × 5 cm (2 in × 2 in) are ideal, but difficult to obtain and must be treated with a wood preservative well before use.

Never attempt to drive in a new stake after planting. In the history of gardening, there have

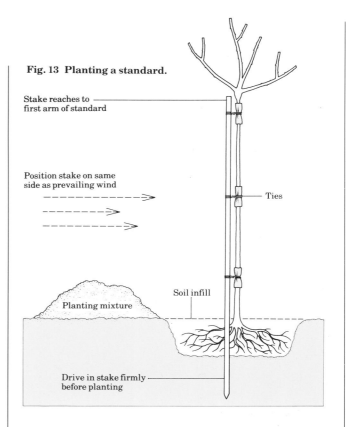

Fig. 13 Planting a standard.

Stake reaches to first arm of standard

Position stake on same side as prevailing wind

Ties

Soil infill

Planting mixture

Drive in stake firmly before planting

been far too many smashed tree heads caused by over-enthusiasm with a heavy hammer!

When the hole to receive the standard is prepared, drive the supporting stake in and position the standard to confirm that the stake will support the plant to just below the union of the first break (the lowest position it was budded). Once the standard has been planted and well firmed, the operation is completed by securing the stem to the stake with a tree tie.

Planting a containerized rose

In some inhospitable climates and soils, where autumn or early spring planting is impossible, containerized roses can be used to great advantage in the late spring and early summer. Care

must be taken to ensure plants are well watered *before* planting. The plant will arrive in a rigid pot or plastic container: whichever mode, care must be taken to remove the plant without disturbing the roots. Use a planting mixture as an added bonus, firm the plant well in and water regularly at least twice a week until the plant is well established.

Planting a rose in a pot

The concept of growing a rose in a pot, tub or trough has an appealing quality which will repay handsome dividends if the limitations of these types of plant are borne in mind. The rose by its very nature is a deciduous plant which, unless grown in a protected area (greenhouse or conservatory), can only be expected to flower for about five months of the year at the maximum. Secondly, irrespective of its type (bush, patio, etc.) the root system can be quite extensive and does not take kindly to the constriction of a confined area. Thirdly, plants will grow well in certain environments and the rose is no different to any other plant.

Ideally a Floribunda of bushy habit, a patio rose, a miniature or even a standard propagated with these types planted in a semi-porous earthenware container, is the best choice.

The container, of whatever construction, must be large enough to give the plant a good root run. This will require a minimum capacity of 1 cu ft and the depth should be greater than the breadth. The soil must be a high-quality potting compost.

Although large clay pots are best, very good results have been obtained with large wooden half-barrels. Whatever the container, remember that all plants in this situation require constant

◀ **'The Fairy' is an ideal rose to plant in a container or in the front of a mixed border. It has a semi-lax habit and a long flowering period.**

maintenance, must have ample drainage, and be situated away from any draught. If a standard or climbing rose is contemplated, then there must be ample provision for good staking or some form of trellis.

Soil sickness and replacement

The popularity of the rose in the last 30 years has created a problem which we have been aware of for some time but only recently addressed. It is the difficulty of worn-out rose soils and the practicality of replacing them. Most environments will support a variety of plants, seemingly indefinitely; however since the agricultural revolution, farmers have been aware that the same crop grown repeatedly in the same field will produce a deteriorating yield and in the course of time be non-productive. Garden soils will of course react in a similar fashion (this phenomenon is only too apparent in the vegetable garden).

That a soil can become exhausted growing a particular genus has become painfully apparent in the matter of roses. Basically what happens is that a rose or a rose bed may be productive, healthy and well grown for many years. The crunch comes when that position or bed is cleared and a fresh plant or plants are put in place, and then fail. The soil appears to have built up numbers of antibodies which preclude replanting with the same genus.

The gardener has several options. He can plant something quite different, he can grass the area over and create fresh beds or he can replace the soil.

In small gardens the latter can be done quite simply by introducing fresh soil from a different part of the garden that has not supported a rose for four years. In larger areas the beds are refurbished by removing the soil by mechanical means and introducing a new medium.

· 5 ·

The Mysteries of Pruning

Many newcomers to gardening are dissuaded from growing roses because of the aura of mystery which surrounds their pruning. In reality, this is a simple exercise. Most horticulturalists are aware of the necessity to control roses by pruning but few are aware of the techniques and the reason why this has to be done.

The modern rose, which has evolved over many years, is a sophisticated plant which at no time in its development has given of its maximum without judicious cultivation and pruning.

The simplest roses, the species or wild roses, require absolutely no attention whatsoever; indeed to control this type of rose can create ugly and unsightly growth. Modern roses, on the other hand, will survive without pruning but will produce a sub-standard plant.

Why prune?

Pruning is the removal, on a seasonal basis, of non-productive wood, the presence of which would deter the plant from giving of its best. The majority of modern roses are recurrent flowering. The flower-producing wood quickly becomes obsolete and is an encumbrance to the further development and production of a well-shaped plant and a continuity of flower.

When to prune

In the normal course of events, pruning time is in the early spring of the year when the plant is in a frost-free environment. Many theories have been propounded on the methods of pruning and as the rose is further developed there will be many more. There are no set rules, rather a series of commonsense observations. Never attempt to cut wood if it is in a frozen condition. A night frost following a day's pruning can do no harm. In climates where the winter is relatively mild, do not cut back (prune) roses in the autumn as this will encourage immediate new growth which will be damaged in any hard weather. However, tall bushes should be trimmed, removing about a third of the autumnal growth.

Modern advice is suggesting that very hard pruning, which has been very fashionable since the turn of the century, is now outmoded and there is a general consensus of opinion that most recently bred varieties of bush roses will give better results if more wood is left on the plant. Indeed there is even a school of thought that positively encourages the coarse removal of top wood, leaving the rest of the fabric of the plant intact. This procedure is not new but has caused much comment as it has always been assumed that an accummulation of scrubby growth at the base of the tree was an impediment. Experience now tells us that although this is perfectly true, as the plant ages the burden of so much non-productive wood will work to its detriment.

Good pruning is always completed by tidying up and spraying with a comprehensive fungicide.

Pruning tools (Fig. 14)

● *Secateurs* are the most important tool that a rosarian owns. The introduction of the modern 'side by side' secateurs has revolutionized the art into a pleasurable activity. A good clean cut without bruising the fabric of the plant has always been considered essential and until relatively recently the only method of doing this was with a good strong pruning knife.

There are many brands on the market but without doubt the finest make which is readily available in most rose-growing areas in the world are the range of secateurs made by the well-known Swiss firm of Felco. Although the basic principle is the same, no matter what the pattern is used, there are many varied designs to suit the gardener, ranging from a heavy professional model to a lighter one for more delicate and smaller hands. There are even models available for the left-handed person. They require little maintenance and the blades are quickly replaced if damaged.

● *Longarms or parrot-nose secateurs* are useful when extra strength is needed. The extended handle will enable big stems to be removed without fear of injury.

● *A pruning saw* can be a great help. A well-designed model will fold like a knife to stow away when not in use. Occasionally, particularly in the bigger shrubs and climbers, a very thick branch has to be removed and this is the only instrument that will reach into confined spaces.

● *A carborundum stone* is invaluable, though well-cared-for high-quality tools rarely require much sharpening.

● *Knife.* A conscientious gardener, particularly a rose grower, will feel undressed if he does not have a sharp knife in his pocket at all times. Any

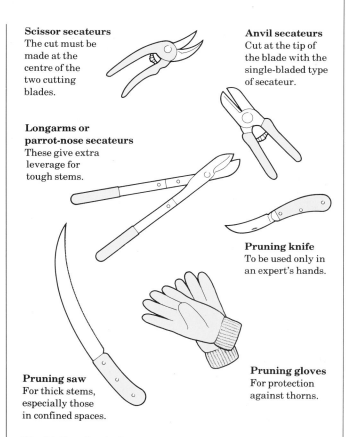

Scissor secateurs
The cut must be made at the centre of the two cutting blades.

Anvil secateurs
Cut at the tip of the blade with the single-bladed type of secateur.

Longarms or parrot-nose secateurs
These give extra leverage for tough stems.

Pruning knife
To be used only in an expert's hands.

Pruning saw
For thick stems, especially those in confined spaces.

Pruning gloves
For protection against thorns.

Fig. 14 Pruning tools.

cutting tool must be kept clean and wiped occasionally with a spirit base to sterilize and prevent the possible spread of virus diseases through the plant sap.

● *Good leather pruning gloves* are essential. Many people loathe wearing them but they are a necessity, particularly when handling old plants where the thorns can cause nasty wounds if neglected.

Good tools are expensive but a worthy investment, and the roses will benefit.

Rose hips are a great attraction to birds in the garden but care must be taken not to allow these varieties to be dead headed.

The *rugosa* family are justifiably famous for the quality and fruitfulness of the large bright red hips which will give colour to the garden in the autumn.

Pruning new plants

There appears to be a general assumption that rose bushes do not require pruning in the spring following planting. This is quite wrong and can only be assumed to have gained credence because of the relatively small size of the plant. Most nurseries cut their plants down before despatch in order to reduce the cost of carriage. In effect this means that bush roses will arrive with about 45 cm (15 in) of top growth, and shrubs and climbers about 60 cm (24 in). No harm is caused by this practice but the bush has not been pruned! The average Hybrid tea or Floribunda will have to be cut down further in the early spring to about 15 cm (6 in). In many respects this first pruning is more important than any subsequent exercise. Cut, if possible, to an outside eye or bud. Shrubs and climbers will require no further attention other than the removal of any dead wood. Standard bush roses will have to be pruned in a similar manner to a bush.

Remember that newly planted bushes will require re-treading in the spring after the loosening effects of frost on newly dug soil.

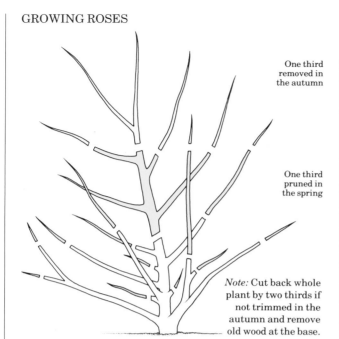

One third removed in the autumn

One third pruned in the spring

Note: Cut back whole plant by two thirds if not trimmed in the autumn and remove old wood at the base.

Fig. 15 Pruning a bush rose (Floribunda or Hybrid tea)

Pruning established bushes (Fig. 15)

When Floribundas were first marketed there was a popular belief that they did not require such hard pruning as the contemporary Hybrid teas. This may have been true in those early days but modern bushes of any persuasion are now treated equally.

When pruning an established plant, attempt to reduce the plant by about two thirds. Therefore a rose bush whose average height is about 1 m (3 ft) when in full flower will have to be cut down to about 30 cm (1 ft). This recommendation is obviously contrary to the old-fashioned dictum where instructions were given relative to the number of eyes (or buds) that had to be left. Of greater importance is the attention that must be paid to the remaining wood.

All rose bushes will accumulate a certain percentage of old and twiggy fabric and worn-out

· HANDY TIP ·

Although roses are very hardy, they can on occasion be cut down quite severely by frost. This may appear disastrous but very rarely fatal. Do not remove the plant. Cut off the damaged wood and almost certainly new growth will appear from the crown, though it may well be in late spring before this happens.

stumps and it is important that this is removed. Ideally this should be done first, leaving the strong shoots to be reduced with impunity. Pruning a rose is in reality the removal of old and decrepit wood, the continued presence of which causes stress to the plant and in addition will harbour latent fungus spores.

In many gardens the plants are trimmed back in late autumn by about one third to reduce wind damage. This is good practice and reduces the incidence of 'rocking' during the winter months which can cause fatalities. As a rule of thumb, if this procedure is practised it will mean that about half the remaining wood is pruned in the spring.

Pruning patios and miniatures

The increased popularity of this type of rose has required some thought on the maintenance in the more intimate areas of the garden where these types are grown. They must be pruned in exactly the same way as the ordinary bush, bearing in mind that the remaining wood should be in proportion to the mature plant, and greater attention is paid to removing old and rubbishy material, and dead and decaying garden detritus which appears to accumulate in this type of plant. There is a tendency with some of the more vigorous patios to throw up an extra long shoot in the late summer; these may be left slightly longer than the rest of the plant. It is appropriate at this time of the year, when the plants are in containers, to repot with fresh compost.

Pruning climbers and ramblers (Fig. 17)

A well-maintained climber can give much beauty to the garden during the winter months. The architectural disposition of the well-ordered branches give visual interest on even the coldest winter day. Contrary to the treatment of bushes, climbers and ramblers are best pruned and tied up in the late autumn. There are two advantages to be gained: it is much easier to identify old growth at this time of the year and, of greater importance, all the potential flowering wood will be secure to meet the winter gales.

● *Pruning a recurrent-flowering climber* is relatively simple as the main object of the exercise is to shorten back the old flowering wood and to reorganize the disposition of the remaining wood to ensure a good coverage of flower the following year. This type of plant will not produce the extremely vigorous growth familiar in its once-flowering cousins; it is therefore essential to retain as much of the fabric as possible and the majority of the shoots are only heavily deadheaded.

● *Summer-flowering ramblers and climbers* require greater attention. The golden rule is to remember that the good strong growth produced in year one is the source of the best bloom in year two. Care must be taken to retain this type of wood and cut back the old flowering wood to about 5 cm (2 in) of the main stem. Occasionally big old main stems will have to be removed completely. This is best done by releasing the plant from the supporting fabric, (wall, fence, pergola etc.), laying it back, trimming and then tying it back up. Never use plastic string which cuts into branches.

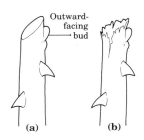

▼ Fig. 16 When pruning, always use good quality, well-sharpened pruning tools. The aim is to make a clean cut just above an outward-facing bud (a). An untidy cut (b) leaves the plant more vulnerable to disease.

Outward-facing bud

(a) (b)

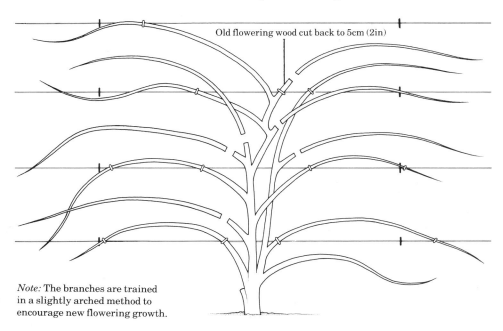

Old flowering wood cut back to 5cm (2in)

▶ Fig. 17 Pruning a climber or rambler.

Note: The branches are trained in a slightly arched method to encourage new flowering growth.

Pruning shrubs

A good rule of thumb with the majority of shrubs is to leave them strictly alone apart from heavily deadheading the old flowering shoots and only 'attack' them when absolutely necessary. This however is not always possible or even wise and therefore some guidance is required.

● *Specie or wild roses* certainly should be left alone. They are natural plants collected from the wild which have survived for many years with no maintenance. Nevertheless this type of plant will occasionally require some form of control and this can be achieved by occasionally cutting out one or stems at the base. This will encourage new growth and allow light into the base. Never shorten stems, as this will produce ugly, unnatural growth.

● *Summer-flowering shrubs* come within the category of old garden roses and can be controlled in two seasons of the year. Summer pruning of the albas, centifolias, gallicas and damasks can produce very satisfactory results. Quite simply, immediately the plant has finished flowering (usually in mid-summer), rather than deadhead, completely remove a proportion of the older flowering branches (about one third) in a bold fashion. This will encourage a rapid re-growth of new wood, providing a plentiful source of flower the following season.

● *Recurrent or remontant flowering shrub roses* should be treated rather like outsize Floribundas, which is what they are. Cut back the flowering wood in the spring – heavily deadheading it may be called – retaining a shape to the plant. In addition, take the opportunity to use the longarms (see page 47) to cut out any old scrubby wood as it accumulates. Many of the modern shrubs are quite capable of producing an autumnal flush to equal the summer contribution if heavily deadheaded and a mid-summer boost of rose fertilizer is applied.

Pruning standards

Pruning a standard of whatever type is relatively simple and many of the rules that relate to the relevant bush variety apply equally when grown as a standard. Cutting back old flowering wood and removing scrubby growth is important. Producing a good shape is probably even greater. Ensure that the finished plant is broader than it is higher. This will give a better shape when in flower. Although the stake and tie should have been checked in the autumn, it is well to repeat the exercise in the spring.

● *Shrub and weeping standards* must be deadheaded and allowed to grow naturally. The weepers will want the very old flowering wood removed but the shrubs are best allowed to grow naturally.

Pruning ground cover

If allowed to grow naturally ground cover roses require little maintenance other than deadheading. They will sometimes produce upright shoots which must be left strictly alone as they will naturally arch and sprawl as they come into flower.

Pruning a rose, whatever the type of variety, method of cultivation or position in the garden, is simply a method of controlling a plant to produce bloom to the maximum effect. It is a means of reducing the stress on the tree in order that it can do this effectively. Spring pruning can also be the occasion to tidy the rose beds. Remove any dead or decaying material, lightly hoe the surface but do not dig the ground around rose plants, apply a spring fertilizer, mulch the beds and spray with good all-round fungicide and aphicide.

'Iceberg' has been described as the ultimate in free-flowering Floribundas and has no equal, particularly as a standard. Cutting back old flowering wood and removing scrubby growth are important to keep it looking at its best.

· 6 ·

Looking After Your Roses

There are few areas in the garden that do not require some form of maintenance during the year, whether it is mowing the lawn, sweeping the patio or generally removing the debris that appears to accumulate. Roses and rose beds are no different in that respect. They are not very demanding and a few moments once a week will suffice to maintain an orderly regime.

Suckers (Fig. 18)

The majority of new roses purchased are propagated on a rootstock. That means that their root system is a different type of rose. This may not become apparent until pale green shoots appear from below ground level, looking more like a briar than the plant you had hoped to see. There was an old wives' tale that this extraneous growth, which we will call suckers, could be identified by the pale green growth and the seven leaflets. Unfortunately this is not exactly true because most ramblers and climbers, some patios and miniatures and all ground cover roses have seven leaflets. Fortunately the stock that rose growers now use (*R. laxa*) has been selected because one of its characteristics is a reluctance to throw these suckers.

Identifying suckers is simple if it is understood that they will only grow from *below* the position on the stock from which the cultivar is budded. A rose cannot 'revert' but sometimes, usually through ignorance or neglect, the root system will do its own thing – that is, the sucker grows strong enough to prevent the cultivar from developing. The process of eliminating this unwanted extraneous growth is called 'suckering'.

The secret of containing this nuisance is to remove suckers as they appear. Sometimes they will occur some distance away from the tree and are removed by easing the soil and gently pulling them up to reveal a length of stem; a good tug will then remove them completely, together with the node they were growing from. Other times they become apparent growing through the middle of the bush, which entails removing some of the soil to reveal their origin, which must then be removed with a sharp instrument. Suckers are readily identified on standard stems below the budding area and are easily rubbed off before they become too big. It is a comforting thought that many ground covers and miniatures are now grown on their own roots which precludes this annoying complaint.

Blind shoots

There is always disappointment when some shoots appear blind, that is with no flower bud in early summer. Many theories have been suggested as to the cause of this phenomenon, linking it to certain strains of breeding. The probability is that late frosts or a sudden drop in temperature are the main causes. Blind shoots never appear on the second flush of flower.

The remedy is not to prune too soon or feed too early. These barren shoots should be cut down half way and will then produce healthy flower buds.

Whatever plant is being tidied up the important factor to remember is to collect the dead heads/prunings and not allow them to clutter the garden, as this will only encourage pests and diseases.

Obviously varieties of rose, usually species, which are being grown for their harvest of hips, must be left alone. On the other hand, extremely floriferous varieties, particularly Floribundas, may need dead-heading several times in the season.

Weak necks and balling
Occasionally in warm wet weather the blooms, particularly of the very large Hybrid teas, appear to turn brown and rot off before they have had a chance to develop. This is called 'balling' and occurs in warm wet weather and an attack of mildew; it is difficult to avoid if climatic condi-

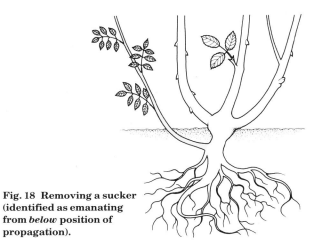

Fig. 18 Removing a sucker (identified as emanating from *below* position of propagation).

tions are conducive. Sometimes the neck of the rose immediately below the immature flower appears to go mouldy and rot. These malfunctions usually appear on the same type of rose.

Although persistent rainy conditions and humidity are the direct cause of these defects it is also a symptom of roses being grown too soft, probably through over-enthusiasm to give the plant too much nitrogen. The long-term remedy is to raise the level of potash in the early spring dressing, but much good can be done by spraying with a mildew specific. The offending heads should be cut off and added to the compost heap.

Deadheading
Sadly when roses fade they are not a pretty sight and the tidy gardener much prefers that the flower heads are removed. Many are content to do a quick snap off of the head to remove the offending old bloom, but to the more industrious and painstaking gardener deadheading is a science that has to be taken seriously. The principle is to remove the old flower head, together with the part of the stem that cannot be expected to produce a continuity of flower – usually about 50 per cent of the supporting stem. The effect is two-fold: the old flower which in many varieties would normally produce a hip is removed, thus preventing a development which would deter a second flush of flower; but of greater importance, the buds immediately below the old flower are barren, or at best only capable of producing poor quality bloom. In short, dead-heading is a method of cleaning a plant in summer to make it more productive in the autumn.

● *Summer pruning* can be likened to this exercise but is more closely associated with the removal of old flowering wood on a summer-

55

flowering variety or once-flowering rose. Here the principle is to encourage fresh growth in order that the next season's flowering wood is formed.

Cutting back for winter

A modern rose is expected to produce growth throughout the growing season. As a deciduous plant it will rarely retain much foliage after the first heavy frosts. A recurrent-flowering rose will do all these things but also produce flower until late autumn. There is a great temptation once the flowering season comes to a close, to cut back all the extraneous growth it makes for a tidy-looking garden. This is a good principle and has great merit. Some plants will grow very tall and ungainly in the late autumn and barely mature enough to produce flower. It is this type of growth that must be cut back to reduce the windage on

◀ Standards can give an added dimension to the rose garden and relieve an otherwise flat aspect, but they must be well staked and secured.

▶ Weeping standards are spectacular and this plant of 'Dorothy Perkins' is a very good example of the type which will grow naturally without artificial persuasion.

the plant. In most temperate climates frost rarely damages roses, but a plant that has too much top to it will rock in the wind and fatal damage can occur to the root system. In effect, reduce these plants by one third and remove the other third when they are pruned in the spring.

Shrub roses and standards can be similarly trimmed but to a lesser degree. Climbers and ramblers can sometimes be forgotten. From mid-summer onwards many of them are producing vast amounts of wood which are invaluable and must be retained at all cost. The judicious use of soft string to secure this growth as it develops is of primary importance. Never tie in this young wood too tightly or it will be damaged.

Dead and heavily diseased plants must be marked for renewal and if necessary removed immediately. One final point: towards the end of the growing season remove old dead branches which are much easier to identify while the newer wood is a brighter green, and remember that this type of wood will blunt good secateurs very quickly, so use a saw or longarms.

Mulching

The control of weeds and the necessity to preserve a modicum of healthy soil management is of great importance during the growing months. This can be achieved by giving the rose beds/plants a mulch. Mulching involves covering the soil around the plants, usually with an organic content, to contain the moisture and suppress the weeds. There are many mediums, peat (or peat substitute), ground bark in many forms, lawn-mowing cuttings and good old-fashioned well-rotted farmyard manure. The first two of these are very good weed supressants but have very little food value; the other two are very good feeds, wonderful conservers of moisture but are host to a multitude of weeds. Either way, they are best applied when the soil is moist and as early in the season as possible.

Weed control

There is an old country saying that if the soil cannot grow weeds then it will never grow anything else and realistically this is very true. There are nevertheless some useful remedies that will reduce this natural problem. Farmyard manure is the most valuable source of nutrient to the soil but is also the finest agent to propagate weeds. This can be remedied by composting it well by stacking, making sure it is well rotted before application.

In a new garden identify the dominant weeds and do not allow them to flower and seed. When preparing new rose beds, clean the soil of any perennial roots before planting. A light hoe will control most seedlings, provided they are caught at an early stage.

● *Weedkillers* are readily available but must be used judiciously. The majority are contact sprays that are absorbed by the offending weed and control is very good; remember, however, that with one or two exceptions they are equally efficient demolishing rose plants! Other sprays and powders are applied to the soil and subsequently absorbed by the roots. They are very successful, but again follow the directions to avoid disappointment.

Weeds can sometimes be a valuable source of compost. Never use this type of material if it has been killed with a weedkiller. The dead fabric has a nasty habit of absorbing the effective chemical which can be released if used as a mulch. Grass clippings are also a valuable source of compost if broken down properly, but again not if the lawn has recently been treated with a weedkiller.

Feeding

The rose, like any other plant, will give better results if fed properly. It will also be much healthier, particularly if it receives the correct nutrients at the right time of year. Although the rose does not possess a coarse appetite, it nevertheless is demanding at certain times and neglecting this important seasonal obligation will result in poor growth and disease.

Potash comes very high on the list of essential nutrients in a good rose fertilizer. Never be persuaded to pick up a cheap fertilizer, particularly in rural areas where they are probably more appropriate for cereals. The proportion of nutrients is quite wrong and will encourage coarse growth.

The secret of feeding your rose plants is to give a well-balanced fertilizer according to the recommended manufacturer's instructions. The first application should be immediately after pruning but before any spring mulch. A second dressing is advised immediately before the first flush of flower but never after mid-summer.

· FEEDING PROGRAMME ·

The important factor when feeding roses is that any fertilizer, no matter what the constituents, will take time to break down to become available to the plant. It is therefore not advisable to apply anything after mid-summer as this will cause late autumn growth and an inability for the plant to harden off and be in a fit state to face the hard winter weather.

Season	Feeding task
Late winter	Mulch with well-rotted farmyard manure or similar compost, taking care the plants are free of weeds and the soil is moist. Give a dressing of 60 g (2 oz) per square metre (sq yard) of sulphate of potash.
Early spring	Immediately after pruning (bush roses) give a good dressing of a comprehensive garden fertilizer (according to the producers' instructions).
Late spring/ early summer	Apply extra feed to roses grown for *exhibition purposes* with dried blood.
Early summer	On the formation of the new flowering buds give a good dressing of a specific rose fertilizer.

Organic manure, if available, must be well prepared and applied in late winter but remember to dress with potash 60 gm (2 oz) to the square metre (yard) beforehand. Some calcareous (chalky) soils are difficult to grow roses on and a foliar feed with a sequestrated formulation will help. Other foliar feeds can be applied with fungicides and aphicides as a cocktail.

Watering

The root system of a rose plant is extremely vigorous and is quite capable of reaching considerable depths. This makes it relatively independent of heavy rainfall, even in the summer months. However these deep roots cannot take up growth nutrients which are just below the surface. The dilemma is whether to water and risk making the plant dependent on a surface-rooting system, or allow the roots to search for water. It is now common practice for rose nurseries to be equipped for irrigation to cater for very dry summers and newly planted stock, but it is not to be recommended in domestic gardens.

Watering is a long and tedious process and can produce a dependent plant, unable to withstand winter frosts. There are nevertheless two situations where it is advisable to water. New container-grown roses planted in the spring or summer must be well watered in and occasional applications for the first four or five weeks. The other problem area where watering is of great benefit is newly planted climbers and ramblers. These occasionally, particularly when planted in a dry situation such as against a wall or a tree stump, have a habit of remaining in a seemingly moribund condition. A very heavy watering – some five or six large buckets at ten-day intervals – will wake them up.

Never allow your plants to become dependent on constant watering.

◄ Top left: Black spot is easy to identify and can cause rapid defoliation of affected plants. Sound feeding and early spraying is the best treatment.

▲ A plant suffering from an attack of rust has leaves with minute red postules that turn black with age and must be sprayed immediately to prevent the disease spreading.

◄ Leaf-rolling sawfly is the cause of these peculiar leaf formations which are probably more unsightly than creating any permanent damage.

· 7 ·
Rose Clinic

A healthy plant is a happy plant. The number of fatalities that occur when roses are despatched from the nurseries or collected from garden centres is very small and is usually caused in the handling and planting. Plants that have been allowed to dry out in transit have a great handicap. The remedy is therefore never plant a tree with dry roots; soak them if necessary in water before planting (an hour is quite long enough).

The modern rose has a greater resistance to disease than some of its forbears but it is not good practice to plant in an environment that is hostile. By that we mean old rose ground, water-logged soil, dry conditions and probably the worst scenario of the lot, in association with other diseased plants. It is unfair to expect a plant to survive in a garden that already has in it an old rambler prone to mildew or a black spot-ridden freak of yesteryear.

A well-balanced food regime is of primary importance. Too much nitrogen will produce sappy soft growth which is an invitation to disease. Greater resistance can be encouraged by growing a hard tree with a good application of potash (see page 59) in the early spring. The elimination of dead and decaying wood, diseased leaves and garden rubbish is a great help. An overall winter spray may be able to clean up a garden but is probably used to greater advantage in the greenhouse.

How long will a rose live?
There are several considerations that will determine the life of a rose. There is a general consensus that a properly maintained rose, fed and pruned in a rational way, will live about 15 years. This is a rough guide but can easily be proved to be misleading. In Europe a bed of rose bushes can be expected to give satisfaction for some ten years but the first fatality will occur within about six. This is simply because factors outside the gardener's control can have some bearing on the plant's longevity. A household pet or visiting rabbit, which uses the corner plant as a staging post, is not helpful; a window cleaner may be clumsy with a ladder; or over-enthusiasm with a lawnmower can wreak terrible damage. Other culprits are as follows.

● *Frost* In the majority of temperate climates where roses are popular, it is extremely rare for a plant to be killed by frost; it may be cut down but it is resilient enough to grow again from the base. In the UK, for example, there have been only three winters in the last 50 years that have experienced real rose-killing temperatures.

● *Bad drainage* can cause great problems and a combination of heavy clay and a wet winter can wreak terrible damage.

● *Awkward soils*. The soil is probably the greatest factor allied to specific varieties and colour types.

Copper colours are not supposed to like sand and chalk, some of the vermilions only like cold soils – there are many theories. Light sandy soils are what are called hungry and roses grown in those conditions require quantities of organic food.

Chalky soils (alkaline) are an absolute anathema (the ideal pH is 6.5) to most roses but it is not impossible and the use of sequestrated iron as a foliar feed has yielded promising results.

● *Disease* is the greatest factor determining the longevity of the rose. Repetitive defoliation which occurs with attacks of black spot is extremely debilitating; rust has much the same effect.

DISEASES

In the plant world, as in so many other facets of modern life, prevention of disease is much the better method of organizing a garden than expensive cures.

Black spot

The appearance of large black spots on rose leaves from mid-summer onwards, followed by rapid defoliation, is the nightmare of all rose lovers. Black spot is a fungus disease that can cause great damage to rose plants because of the defoliation of the affected leaves. The introduction of 'clean air' has exacerbated the situation.

On a precept that prevention is better than cure, a healthy regime can be encouraged by observing a few simple rules:

1. Keep the proportion of old and dead wood down to a minimum at all times.
2. A good mulch can maintain a high level of moisture in the soil, which appears to be beneficial.
3. Spray immediately after pruning previously infected trees and the surrounding soil.

4. Repeat this spraying in early summer, once the flower buds have been formed, and repeat in mid and late summer.

● *Chemical sprays* Modern deterrents are systemics, that is sprays that are absorbed by the plant. To get a good coverage the foliage must be thoroughly wetted all over. There are several chemicals now available under a variety of trade names. The main active constituents are bupirimate, triforine, myclobutanil and pirimiricarb. Whichever formulation is used, be careful to follow the manufacturer's instructions. Sprays are most effective if applied in the cool of the evening and not in bright sunshine.

Mildew

An attack of mildew is recognized by the young foliage assuming a grey powdery mould on the flower buds and leaves, but there is no defoliation. It is an unsightly disease but fortunately does not have a debilitating effect on the plant. In common with black spot, it is encouraged by the over-enthusiastic application of nitrogen and is common in some varieties, while others appear to have a certain immunity.

Experience has shown that the disease is more prevalent with a combination of heat, humidity and cold nights. There was also some evidence that scented roses were prone to mildew, but modern breeding has solved that problem.

Apart from growing mildew-free varieties and avoiding the old ramblers which are very prone, the basic strategy is to allow plants plenty of light and air without overcrowding. The majority of black spot sprays will also control mildew.

● *Downy mildew* should not be confused with the powdery form. It rarely appears on garden plants and is usually associated with greenhouse varieties, and complications caused by various forms of malfunction of propagating methods.

There are other maladies which can attack roses but fortunately none as significant as black spot and mildew and can be avoided by eliminating frail varieties and selecting roses that are happy in your part of the world.

Rust

This is an insidious disease which can attack a rose plant in similar circumstances to black spot. The symptoms are the appearance of small bright red postules on the underside of leaves which eventually turn black. The top surface has bright yellow spots/dots and eventually the plant loses its leaves. This affliction has been known to kill a plant and consequently affected plants used to be eliminated.

Research into prophylactics on economic plants has produced a very reliable control and spraying with myclobutanyl has been eminently successful.

Canker

This is not easily identified until a branch or in some instance a whole tree collapses, usually when the plant is in full growth. Appearing as a discoloured area at the base of a stem or plant, it is usually introduced by a wound caused by a hoe or similar mechanical damage. The infected area gradually spreads to encircle the stem and the branch or tree eventually collapses, though fortunately this is a very rare occurrence.

Any infected material must be removed and burnt and the implements wiped with a surgical spirit before being used again.

Viruses

Although prevalent in the US these are not of great consequence and rarely debilitating. The symptoms are varied but usually a pale yellow veining (vein banding rose mosaic) will appear in late spring. Weedkiller damage can sometimes have the same effect. The other virus is line pattern rose mosaic, which actually looks quite pretty and appears in early summer. Neither is very worrying but can spread very easily if secateurs are not sterilized after handling the infected varieties.

Honey fungus

If a plant collapses during the late summer and there are toadstools growing close by, then the chances are that honey fungus is present. This can be diagnosed by digging the soil and looking for the presence of 'boot lace'-looking strands of the fungus. This is usually fatal to the plant. Remove and burn all traces of the root system of the affected plant, drench the area with one of the honey fungus chemicals and replant.

· RULES FOR CHEMICAL SPRAYING ·

- NEVER keep any surplus mixed spray.
- NEVER keep any sprays in unmarked containers.
- NEVER use sprays from a farmer. (The concentrates are usually quite different to those for domestic use.)
- ALWAYS use protective gloves when mixing and handling garden chemicals.

PESTS

In spite of the tremendous advances made in rose breeding, nobody has produced a rose which is resistant to the depredations of certain pests, which appear to obtain great delight living off the sap, devouring leaves and generally using the plant as a refilling station. Fortunately, apart from one or two uninvited guests, they are more of a nuisance than a real threat.

Greenfly

This is the commonest of these predators. They appear in large numbers in late spring to feed on the sap of tender shoots and can very quickly reduce the vigour of this new wood. Yellow, green or black, they can wreak havoc in a very short time.

Many gardeners swear by their own remedies such as soapy water, pyrethrum (for the organic gardener), or a good thunderstorm. However modern systemic sprays are super efficient and a good wetting with a spray based on hepterophos is absolutely lethal to greenfly. Read the manufacturer's instructions carefully and never spray in bright sunshine.

Leaf-rolling sawfly

This can cause unsightly damage and is usually associated with old gardens and plants in wooded areas. The leaves appear to curl lengthways but no permanent damage is done to the plant. The cause is a fly which deposits its eggs on the young leaf, so causing a chemical reaction which then produces the curl.

The remedy is to mark the infected plants, pull off the injured leaves and the following spring, on a warm day, spray the soil below these plants with fenitrothion before the emerging fly can crawl back up the plant and plant its eggs.

Tortrix moth and lacky moth

Both these use young rose leaves as a harbour for depositing their eggs and the subsequent hatchings to produce caterpillars.

Leaf miners and leaf hoppers

These appear to feast on young leaves and again their progeny appear to be voracious. A great mistake is made in assuming that sprays specifically recommended to control aphids will also kill caterpillars. This is quite wrong. Quite the most effective deterrent is pirimiphosmethel.

Japanese beetles and other leaf-cutting bugs

Although these two intrusive predators have a high profile and appear to devour copious quantities of leaves, they very rarely have a long-term effect on the plant. The remedies are various but inevitably resort to human intervention in some shape or form.

The best and simplest way to control Japanese beetle is remove them using a pair of gloves and a bucket of hot water!!

Thrips

These are one of the most irritating insects both bodily to the gardener and intrusively to the rose bloom. They are known also as thunder flies. Minute flying insects, they have perfected the habit of pervading the innermost reaches of the rose (and the gardener). They have a penchant for pale-coloured roses where they appear to nibble emerging flowers and create unsightly dark edges and mottled disfigured petals.

The one consolation is that they are of a temporary nature and disappear as quickly as they appear with a turn in the weather. In very bad infestations a spray with pyrethrium or nicotine will give some protection.

OTHER PROBLEMS

Frost damage

This can occur in the spring in areas where late frosts are a problem. This can manifest itself in extreme unseasonal temperatures by the foliage appearing scorched. Never cut this damaged material down. Rather allow the plant to produce new growth naturally and the damaged fabric will fade away. Cool nights in the late spring will sometimes cause blind shoots to appear. Cut these back as for deadheading, and new flowering shoots will appear almost immediately as a sign of the plant's recovery.

Weedkiller damage

The symptoms of weedkiller damage are easy to identify. The young growths appear starved, twisted and malformed, producing pinnate leaflets. Over-enthusiastic use of weedkillers in the garden is a main cause. So, too, is carelessness about hygiene: the failure to clean watering cans and spraying equipment that have previously been used for treating lawns and paths. It is good practice to use equipment specifically for this purpose, but if necessary clean all utensils that have been used with hot soda water.

Cuttings from lawns that have been treated may be absentmindedly used to contribute to compost heaps or as a direct mulch, a dangerous procedure that has virtually ruled out this valuable source of mulch in the garden. In rural areas and in gardens where large playing fields are close by, great damage can be caused by drift, although modern spraying units are designed to prevent this occurring. This has been known to happen within distances of two or three miles of a garden.

Fortunately the majority of plants affected in this way will recover quite quickly, the damaged foliage will disappear and the plant will flower again without too much of an interruption. Do not overfeed in these circumstances. Mild damage is better left to work itself out.

Predators

With the ever-increasing invasion of the countryside by property developers, there is a reluctance for foraging animals to move on. Deer and rabbits regard the succulent stems of roses in the new gardens as a bonus. Many remedies have been suggested and enquiries from local rural communities will produce some fantastic nostrums. Where deer are prevalent fencing is the only real answer, although alarm guns similar to those used for scaring pigeons have been known to be effective. Rabbits also have to be fenced out but this is simpler and cheaper. Moles can easily be trapped.

There are many remedies that are available from garden centres to discourage animals but unfortunately many are unpleasant to handle and may alienate your neighbours as well.

Cats and dogs can do much damage and are the source of much domestic litigation. There are many deterrents which can actually be sprayed on favourite plants.

Birds are not known to damage rose plants, and indeed they can help with their diet of insects.

Two-legged predators have been known to cause great damage through vandalism. Planting a very thorny hedge, particularly one of the rugosas, is a marvellous obstacle!

In spite of these potential problems the rose is an extremely resilient and long-suffering plant that, grown with a modicum of care, should give pleasure for many years. There are many that are 40 years old and more.

· 8 ·

Propagation and Breeding

The majority of new rose plants have been propagated on a root stock. The reason is quite simple: as roses have been selected and bred to greater heights of sophistication, they appear to have lost their ability to produce a root system capable of supporting a vigorous plant and quality flower. The term 'budding' is used to describe how a new plant is produced by this method.

Many varieties of rose can be grown quite easily from cuttings, but they tend to be the older ramblers, species and some of the old garden roses. An anomaly is that some of the very new ground cover roses and miniatures are being grown quite successfully from cuttings and the results would suggest that in the not too distant future the wheel will have turned full circle and budding roses will be a thing of the past. The techniques of budding and growing roses from cuttings are termed 'vegetative propagation'.

Propagating from seed is the method used to produce new varieties of rose, and is called 'hybridizing'. Modern roses have such a polyglot ancestry that it is not possible to grow a variety true from seed. That is why budding or taking cuttings is used to multiply a rose from stock. In essence therefore, rose growers/nurseries are the source for new rose plants available via mail order or from a garden centre. Rose breeders are the hybridists who produce new varieties of rose and with a modicum of success will persuade rose growers to bud and sell them.

BUDDING (Fig. 19)

The principle of propagating a plant by budding or grafting is common with many genus. All fruit trees and many decorative shrubs are increased by these methods.

The stock

Rosa canina (dog rose) was commonly used for the purpose of supplying the stock. They were grown from seed by specialist nurseries and planted out the following spring in endless rows by rose growers. This stock was used for about 150 years but had one important drawback: it produced suckers and was very variable in quality. With an increased awareness of these problems, a different stock was developed and today the majority of varieties are budded on *R. laxa*. This stock is raised in much the same way as the *canina* but produces a very high-quality plant. With an almost complete absence of sucker, it has become very popular. *R. laxa* does, however, have two handicaps: a tendency to rust, and they must also be budded early in the season – certainly by mid-summer. Stocks are available from a few nurseries for amateurs to bud their own plants.

The stocks are planted in the early spring in a well-prepared tilth, in rows about 1 m (3¼ ft) apart and 20 cm (8 in) plant to plant. After firming they require little maintenance, apart from weeding until early summer.

Preparing stocks and bud wood

The stock will grow quite quickly and should be big enough to work on by early summer. The operative part of the plant is called the barrel, that is the stem of the stock immediately below the position the top growth emanates from. Stocks are graded by the diameter and the quality and straightness of the barrel. The soil will have to be cleared away to make the barrel accessible and a wipe with a piece of cloth will produce a nice clean area to work on.

The principle of budding is transferring the bud situated inside the leaf stock of the variety to be propagated into the stock in such a manner that the line of cells underneath the bark of the bud (called the cambium) lies against the similar structure on the stock. Generally this part of the plant is called the sap.

Bud wood is collected by selecting the stem of the variety which is to be budded. In a bush rose it is usually a stem that has just produced a flower. The bark must be hard enough to handle but not too mature or there will be no sap to allow the buds to 'run'. The stick is cut with secateurs, then trimmed, removing the old flowering head together with two or three of the top leaves. The remainder is trimmed to leave about 1 cm (⅜ in) called the leaf stock. At this stage do not remove any thorns.

Sometimes it may be necessary to store these sticks or even transport them some distance. In order to preserve them, wrap them in damp paper or moss at a temperature just above 0°C (32°F). Never stand them in water. When a rose grower wants to grow a new variety he will receive bud wood as described here.

The stick of buds is finally prepared by thorning, a tedious chore which must be done with care. A stick of buds is generally considered to be ripe if the thorns snap off easily, but some

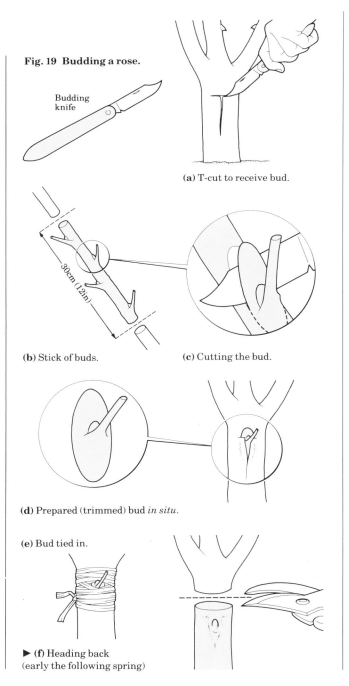

Fig. 19 Budding a rose.

Budding knife

(a) T-cut to receive bud.

30cm (12in)

(b) Stick of buds.

(c) Cutting the bud.

(d) Prepared (trimmed) bud *in situ*.

(e) Bud tied in.

▶ **(f)** Heading back (early the following spring)

67

'Suffolk' is a pretty modern ground cover with a long flowering period which, with its moderate growth, is ideally suited to filling pots and small borders.

varieties can only be dethorned with a sharp knife. Do not attempt to bud in wet weather.

● *Propagating tools* Apart from a hoe to remove the excess soil around the base of the stock the most important tool is the propagator's treasured possession – a budding knife. This instrument must have a very sharp blade of surgical steel quality, with a bone handle tapered at the reverse end to prize open the bark on the stock. A good budder will keep the blade razor sharp with a small carborundum stone, keeping it clean and wiping it down with surgical spirit after each variety, to reduce the incidence of virus. The bud will be secured with wool or a rubber tie.

Budding method
The stock is prepared by slitting the bark to reveal the cambium. It follows therefore that budding can only occur when the sap is running. A cut is made in the form of a T, the horizontal cut first and followed by a vertical which, with the aid of the tapered end of the knife, will reveal the cambium.

The bud is prepared by slicing off a portion of the stem, the bud in the axil of the leaf stock and the bark, with a sliver of wood behind the bark which is removed. The bud is then trimmed to about 1 cm (¼ in) below the leaf stock and inserted in the stock. Although the natural elasticity of the stock will hold the bud *in situ*, raffia or a strip of rubber is normally used to tie it in.

The beginner is advised to practise on pieces of willow before risking his stocks. Practice will make the operation come easy. A professional is expected to bud up to 5,000 a day!!

Heading back
The budding successfully completed, the stock is allowed to heal and the raffia or rubber band will normally perish to leave the bud in position. In some countries with difficult cold conditions, the stock is earthed up for the winter, but it is not a normal practice. Occasionally the bud will grow out immediately after budding, particularly if this was completed early in the season. This is normally cut back when heading.

The final operation is completed the following spring when the top part of the briar is removed, just above the dormant eye, usually called heading back. This is performed with a sharp pair of secateurs and must be a clean cut. Thus a complete root system is left, together with a short stump carrying the dormant eye. As the sap starts to rise the bud will swell, grow and by the

'Bobby James' has the deepest fragrance of all the 'big' ramblers that will clothe pergolas and fences and produce clouds of bloom in high summer.

middle of the summer will be in full flower. When the plant matures in the autumn, it will be ready for planting in its permanent position.

CUTTINGS (Fig. 20)

As previously discussed, many varieties of rose can easily be grown from cuttings. Take a length of stem of the current season's growth in early autumn. With the flowering head or soft growth removed, the remaining wood should be in 23 cm (9 in) lengths. The three lower leaves are removed and the bottom of the stem should be cut across an eye or bud. This eye is gently cut out leaving a heel. The next two buds above are similarly removed, leaving the rest of the stem complete with leaves. Treat the base of the stem with a hormone rooting powder. Plant in a shady part of the garden with only the two top buds above ground level. This cutting will produce a root system with a modicum of top growth and will be ready to move into its permanent position the following autumn.

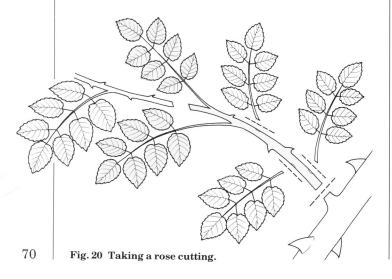

Fig. 20 Taking a rose cutting.

70

PROPAGATING FROM SEED

A new variety of rose can only be obtained by growing from seed. The method of obtaining this seed is called hybridizing. This is a simple exercise requiring parent plants, a modest greenhouse and a basic knowledge of the operative parts of a rose bloom.

● *The flower parts* Basically a rose bloom consists of two major elements which are essential for breeding, (the petals are extraneous to this operation): the male part of the flower is the anther – the part of the bloom which carries the pollen – and this is situated between the petals and the stigma (the centre), which is the female element. The exercise of transferring the pollen onto the stigma is called pollination.

Hybridizing method (Fig. 21)
Hybridizing in most temperate climates must be done in a protected area e.g. a greenhouse, to enable complete control of the operation and give the fertilized hip sufficient time to ripen – which it would not do if 'summer' weather had to be relied upon. The parent plants are either potted up or planted *in situ* in early autumn, pruned very early and encouraged to produce strong flowering shoots but not forced. Heat is not necessary but a frost-free environment in early spring is an advantage.

Immediately colour begins to show on the prospective female flower, the petals are removed to reveal the immature anthers. These are carefully removed with the aid of forceps, leaving no trace of potential pollen-bearing material. This produces what is called an emasculated flower, that is a flower that is wholly female. The immature pollen removed can be retained and used elsewhere when ripe (after 48 hours). The selected male parent (pollen), which when mature

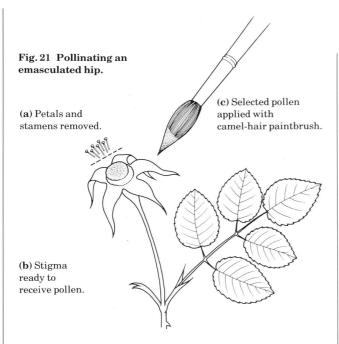

Fig. 21 Pollinating an emasculated hip.

(a) Petals and stamens removed.

(c) Selected pollen applied with camel-hair paintbrush.

(b) Stigma ready to receive pollen.

appears in a floury condition, is applied to the stigma a day after emasculation with a soft brush to complete fertilization. Successfully completed, the hip will develop and is available for harvesting in late autumn. A final but important point: label the hip and note it in your seedling book.

Germination
Rose seed requires considerable skill to achieve a satisfactory germination. The ripe rose hip has to be stratified before sowing, this is picked and submerged in a moist material (vermiculite). Three months later, in late winter, it is subjected to a low temperature (−2°C) for about a week. The seeds are then extracted from the rotting hip and sown in a high quality seed compost about 1 cm (⅜ in) deep. Very little heat is required and, given good germination which is notoriously difficult to achieve, seedlings will appear in about eight weeks. The young plants will rapidly develop to produce a rich show of small blooms.

The skill of the hybridizer is choosing the right parents and selecting the good seedlings which can be grown on, on their own roots or budded. With judicious judgement and not a little luck, a new rose is born. The odds of breeding a commercially successful new variety are astronomical and generally quoted at about 30,000:1!

New roses
Everybody who has enjoyed the excitement of breeding a new rose is fascinated by its development thereon. Potential winners are usually tested by experienced rose growers and, if showing a modicum of success, are distributed to trial grounds at home and abroad. A good rose is recognized very quickly but that is only half the story; finding an appropriate name can be as difficult as breeding. Finally it is possible to obtain protection (patent) and a new rose is launched.

· ROSES BRED BY AMATEURS ·

Although the majority of new roses have been bred by professional hybridizers, there have been quite a number of varieties which have been bred by amateurs. Probably the most famous one was 'Ena Harkness', which was the result of crossing two famous pre-Second World War red roses. Many professionals had endeavoured to be successful with this cross but to no avail. Here are a few of the roses currently available which have been amateur bred:

Baby Bio	Isobel Harkness
Cecily Gibson	Laura Ford
Champagne Cocktail	Lincoln Cathedral
Crimson Showers	Pillar Box
Edith Holden	Peppermint Ice
Frensham	Rebecca Claire
Greenall's Glory	Sheila's Perfume
Harvest Home	St Dunstan's Rose

Note: The Amateur Rose Breeders' Association is a group of enthusiasts interested in this hobby. Their address is at the end of the book (see page 92).

Showing Roses

The village flower fête, the county show or a national occasion like Britain's annual Chelsea Flower Show, are all opportunities to show to your friends, neighbours (or customers) the results of your excellence in growing roses. Although the rose is primarily a garden plant its potential as a cut flower has made it a subject to be used in competition and decoration for many years. Indeed until very recently many were grown simply on their performance on the show bench. Sadly many of these were not particularly good as garden plants and the inevitable publicity which this type of rose gained gave the genus as a whole a bad name. Beware then interpreting show results as an indication of roses to grow, particularly at specialist exhibitions.

Great fun can nevertheless be obtained through showing to your friends the fruits of your labour. With a certain amount of attention to detail you can enjoy not only showing the biggest and the best, but probably of greater importance, plants well grown.

Growing prize-winning blooms

The top exhibitors at a special flower show go to the most extraordinary lengths to produce the most gigantic blooms. Whilst this may not be to everybody's taste, an attention to the basic principles will help. Pruning is of vital importance to allow only the strongest stems to produce poten-tial prize-winning exhibits, cutting back much harder than is normal.

Timing is important and only experience and a little luck will determine this. It can safely be assumed that the longer a bloom has to develop, the better the quality; however a heatwave can throw the most exacting calculations adrift. If serious exhibiting is contemplated, then a series of progressive pruning regimes will cover most eventualities.

The biggest and best blooms are grown with a plentiful supply of well-balanced fertilizer, but augmented with an added boost in the late spring. This is usually achieved with dried blood and fish meal gently hoed in and watered – not the best way of fending off disease but a sure way of getting the biggest and the best.

Hybrid tea bush roses, although technically described as 'large blooms borne singly on a stem', do grow many side shoots. To encourage a greater size, the removal of these must be done as soon as they become visible – generally described as 'disbudding'.

Cut roses

With the exception of specimen plants grown in pots, roses are normally exhibited as cut flowers. The question arises when, where and how. The majority of Hybrid teas will last a considerable length of time if properly conditioned.

A typical prize-winning entry, a bowl of twelve perfect blooms beautifully presented.

The water is of great importance, Ensure that the containers that will receive the bloom are clean – if necessary scrub them out and sterilize them – and make sure they are of sufficient depth to enable the stems to be immersed at least two-thirds of their length.

Cold spring water is quite the best in an ideal world but this is rarely possible to have available. Fortunately there are many preparations that can be added to ordinary tap water, to increase the longevity of the bloom. They are primarily a form of glucose, with soluble traces of various chemicals including an algicide. It is well to remember that the longer a stem stands in water, the less likely it is to take up water. This is because the stem takes up a mixture of water and air and fungi/algae and eventually the stem becomes clogged up and is unable to survive. The solution to the problem, accepting treated water has been used, is to remove a short length of stem about 1 cm (¼ in) with a sharp knife or secateurs when arranging. Indeed some purists recommend cutting stems under water to reduce the introduction of air. Cut the flower when it is torpid i.e. early in the morning, never in hot sun, and then plunge it immediately in water, keep it cool and it will have the potential to decorate the dinner table or stage the best exhibit in the show.

Selection, cutting and transport

The greatest mistake that the majority of novice exhibitors make is failing to cut the bloom early enough. This means, in practical terms, cutting as much as 48 hours before the bloom is scheduled to appear on the show bench. Only from experience can one gauge how far open a bloom has to develop before cutting. Some of the very large varieties with a high petallage will 'stick' for a considerable period and look at their peak for several days.

Immediately the bloom has been cut, plunge it into deep water within minutes. Blooms will grow in size quite rapidly if stored in cool semi-darkness, without appearing to open. If possible travel to a show wet – that is, take the bloom stood in deep water in a florist's bucket. Crumpled newspaper will conveniently control water slopping everywhere. Blooms that appear to be opening too fast can be discouraged by being lightly tied with strands of thick wool.

Some exhibitors have learnt to travel dry, that is the blooms are rolled in newspaper (never use tissue), which should be done carefully but firmly. Either wet or dry, if the bloom is packed loosely it will bruise and damage quickly.

A very large cool box can be used to store roses standing in water apparently indefinitely. How-

ever, there is some skill in this exercise as the optimum temperature is about 2–4°C (36–38°F). A good judge will always spot the tired bloom that has been kept too long in these conditions. The petals assume a woolly texture not unlike blotting paper.

On arrival at the show allow the blooms plenty of air to develop, and of course plunge into water (again prepared) if they travelled dry. Before staging, the exhibitor will have to identify the position of the classes that have been entered and select the potential bloom. The important factor is to allow the blooms to warm up and soften; they will need to be dressed and will damage and bruise if they are in a cold frigid state.

Dressing (Fig. 22)

At animal shows much time is spent by owners grooming and primping. This may not be quite the correct way to describe the preparation of the bloom which in floristry is called dressing. This in essence is the act of gently persuading the bloom to look even more perfect than it really is.

This can be done using a wool tie. If a tie has been used, remove and then with a soft camel hair brush ease two or three of the petals back, care being taken not to cause bruising. A cruder form of this manipulation can be effected by squeezing the petal at the base. This will enhance the bloom very quickly but a good judge will notice this if clumsily performed and pronounce the bloom 'overdressed'.

Outside dirty petals should be removed but be careful not to tear them or again the bloom will lose points.

What are the judges looking for?

A good rose judge will be familiar with the varieties that are being inspected. This means that they will be identified by colour, shape and if necessary foliage. However, rule one is to label each and every variety that is being exhibited. *Know your variety and write legibly.*

Some judges are bemused by sheer size. This may be a contributing factor to a winning bloom, but not at the expense of poor colour quality. A medium-sized high quality bloom with immaculate form should always score more points than a pallid 'turnip'. Many decisions have been made on the quality of foliage, which must be healthy and free from damage. A torn mildewy leaf can spell disaster. The blooms must be as free of damage as possible.

The form of bloom can be described by the classical modern notion of a high centre and reflex petals forming a perfect circle without the centre opening out or 'popped'. The worst form of bloom is what is termed as 'split' – that is, the petals which in perfection should appear beautifully formed and concentric, instead appear to suffer a deformity in the form of a split usually half-way through the blooms development. Judges will deprecate this deformity and will generally give no points at all for a specimen so exhibited.

● *Staging box blooms* is an exact science where perfection and size are the criteria. These very large blooms are frequently controlled by a tie until minutes before the judge's bell sounds, if

Fig. 22 Cutting and dressing a prize bloom for showing.

(a) Bud fresh from garden.

(b) Developing bud with tie.

(c) Bloom (tie removed) before dressing.

(d) Dressed bloom.

Note: Any ties left on will automatically disqualify a bloom.

these are left on and observed the bloom is generally disqualified.

● *Staging stems of Floribundas* and similar cluster-flowered varieties is primarily dependent on the number of blooms and their development. To exhibit a Floribunda with only one or two blooms will not gain much success. To obtain the maximum number of blooms, disbud clusters at a very early stage by removing the leading or centre bud, which is generally well developed before the rest of the spray.

Rose classes (Fig. 23)
The novice exhibitor will be somewhat perplexed by the multiplicity of classes which may be entered and is therefore advised to study the show schedule carefully. Roses are normally shown in three distinct modes: vases, bowls and boxes.

● *Vases* are the simplest form to show blooms. The class usually calls for a number of stems. If the vase is provided by the show organizers, check that it conforms to the schedule. Stabilizing the stems is an easy problem as foam bricks, for example oasis, can be cut to size to fill the containers. This type of material must be well soaked before use and time can be saved by preparing well before staging. This may be before leaving home. This type of material is a far cry from chopped reeds or crumpled wire but must be allowed to absorb treated water naturally. Do not submerge these blocks forcefully, which can cause air pockets to develop with inevitable failures. Arrange the blooms to look well balanced, with a good distribution of colour which can be achieved with a reasonable length of stem – 45 cm (18 in).

● *Bowls* are usually determined by their diameter, usually 15 cm (6 in), 23 cm (10 in) or 30 cm (12 in). Many are supplied with a grid mesh to stabilize the stems, but require considerable skill to arrange. Foam blocks may require wiring down in the bowl, but are easier to handle. Arrange stems in a rounded design. Bowls filled flat are ugly. Both vase and bowl classes are determined by the number of stems which are permitted. Judges will count the number of stems before inspecting the merits of an exhibit.

● *Box classes* are becoming somewhat old-fashioned. Here blooms are presented on short stems about 8 cm (3 in) long, in multiples of 6, 12 etc. in a box formation. The accent is on the size.

Showing is great fun and much enjoyment and many friendships can be obtained by participating.

Fig. 23 Exhibiting modes.

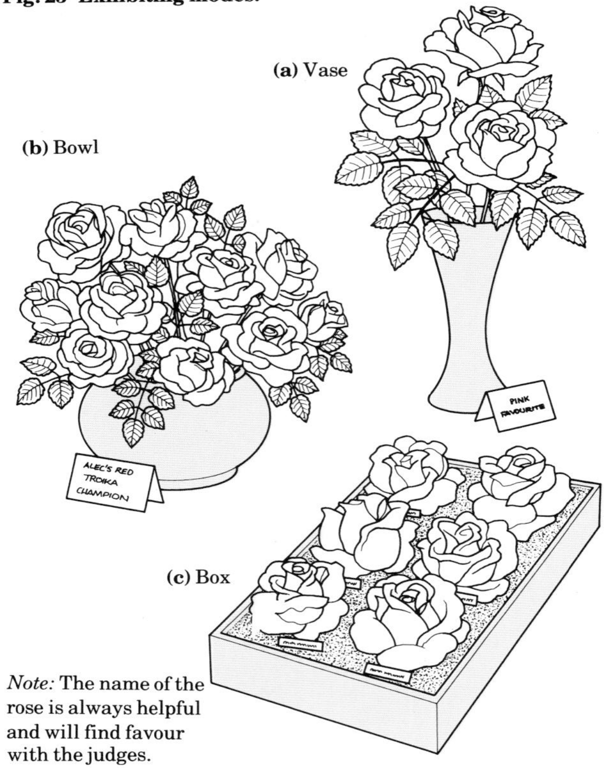

(a) Vase

(b) Bowl

(c) Box

Note: The name of the rose is always helpful and will find favour with the judges.

· 10 ·
Selected Roses for Every Situation

FRAGRANT ROSES

The scent of roses is a personal and often elusive element. A popular fallacy is that few modern roses possess this quality. This may have been true 50 years ago but not today. (For fragrant climbers and ramblers, see page 86.)

Hybrid teas

Alec's Red	Loving Memory
Blessings	Mala Rubinstein
Blue Moon	Paul Sherville
Deep Secret	Prima Ballerina
Double Delight	Royal William
Fragrant Cloud	Super Star
Fragrant Gold	Troika
Fragrant Hour	Whisky Mac
Keepsake	Woods of Windsor

Floribundas

Arthur Bell	Matangi
English Miss	Pineapple Poll
Escapade	Scented Air
Fragrant Delight	Sheila's Perfume
Harvest Fayre	Shocking Blue
Korresia	Southampton
Margaret Merril	Yvonne Rabier

Shrub roses, old and new

Blanc Double de Coubert	Lavender Lassie
Buff Beauty	Louise Odier
Cornelia	Madame Isaac Pereire
Felicia	Madame Pierre Oger
Golden Wings	Paul Neyron
Graham Thomas	Roseraie de l'Haÿ

ROSES FOR EXHIBITION

To grow and exhibit a rose bloom in its perfection is the dream of many gardeners. The rose is primarily a garden plant but some varieties are grown specifically for the show bench, marked here with an asterisk.

Hybrid teas

Admiral Rodney*	Loving Memory
Alec's Red	My Choice
Big Chief*	New Zealand
Big Purple	Peace
Bon Soir*	Peer Gynt
Champion	Perfecta*
City of Bath*	Pink Favourite
Double Delight	Red Devil*
Elina	Royal Highness
Fragrant Cloud	Savoy Hotel
Fred Gibson*	Selfridges
Gavotte*	Silver Jubilee
Grandpa Dickson	Valencia
Keepsake	Wendy Cussons

Floribundas

Anna Livia	Kerryman
Anne Cocker	Matangi
Anne Harkness	Melody Maker
Arthur Bell	Memento
Bucks Fizz	Mountbatten
City of Leeds	Pernille Poulsen
Evelyn Fison	Pink Parfait
Hannah Gordon	Southampton
Iceberg	The Times Rose

77

HYBRID TEA BUSH ROSES

There are currently many hundreds of rose varieties catalogued, leading to considerable bewilderment to the novice rose enthusiast. The lists in this book are compiled to give guidance, indicating the best in each category. Hybrid tea bush roses are probably more confusing than any other type. This select list attempts to provide a guide to the better varieties giving a broad spectrum of habit and colour with a high priority to disease resistance.

Name	Description
Alec's Red	A rich cherry red with large heavily scented blooms on a medium-sized tree.
Alexander	Luminous vermilion flowers with a good length of stem. Big enough to grow as a shrub.
Blessings	The perfect bedding Hybrid tea. The coral salmon blooms are fragrant on a medium-sized plant.
Congratulations	A tall-growing vigorous plant with perfectly shaped blooms reminiscent of florists' flowers. Soft pink with a hint of salmon and a slight fragrance.
Deep Secret	A well scented very dark red.
Double Delight	A bright garish bi-colour, creamy white with carmine edged blooms.

Elina	Clear pale primrose and large. The deep green luxuriant foliage is a perfect foil.
Elizabeth Harkness	A beautiful pastel shade of ivory with a touch of pink and gold. Perfect form.
Fragrant Cloud	Very fragrant large coral scarlet turning crimson as it ages. The perfect answer to the critics who say the modern rose has no scent.
Freedom	Probably the best deep unfading yellow in the garden today. The medium-sized plant is rapidly gaining a reputation for weather resistance and a 'grow anywhere' appeal.
Grandpa Dickson	A pretty lemon yellow medium-sized bloom with a light green foliage.
Ingrid Bergmann	Dark red, very healthy medium bush.
Just Joey	The medium-sized coppery-fawn-buff blooms have a unique character with dark green foliage.
Keepsake	Very large blooms of rose carmine. Equally good in the garden or on the show bench.
Lovers' Meeting	An upright grower. The luminous bright tangerine blooms are good for cutting.
Loving Memory	The large perfectly shaped flowers of crimson scarlet have a slight fragrance. A robust reliable plant.

Pascali	Probably the best pure white Hybrid tea today.
Paul Sherville	An elegant free-flowering rose. The salmon-pink blooms have a good scent.
Peace	A modern old favourite which has survived the test of time. The creamy yellow blooms are flushed with a tint of pink and can produce blooms of a prodigious size.
Piccadilly	The bench mark for bi-colours. A bushy plant with scarlet and yellow blooms.
Polar Star	The large white blooms with a hint of cream are slightly scented.
Rebecca Claire	A reliable coppery orange edged light coral, a good bedding variety.
Remember Me	A deep coppery orange with bronze-coloured foliage. Medium height.
Royal William	The most reliable crimson red rose with a fragrance to be recently introduced.
Rose Gaujard	Carmine and white with a great resistance to disease. Large blooms and plant.
Savoy Hotel	The pastel pink blooms have a perfect shape. The plant is sturdy and of a medium height.
Selfridges	A fragrant tall bright yellow. A prolific producer with good long cutting stems.
Simba	The yellow flowers are borne on a short bush, to make a good bedder.
Tequila Sunrise	The most spectacular of recent introductions. The bright yellow blooms are heavily edged with scarlet and is a good bedder.
Troika	The orange bronze blooms have a keen fragrance. The most reliable variety in this colour.
Valencia	Very large well-shaped blooms of pure apricot with a beautiful fragrance.

· NEW CLASSIFICATIONS ·

The World Federation of Rose Societies published this new classification of roses recently. Although rarely used professionally, it does put the many rose types into a logical sequence.

Modern garden roses

● NON-CLIMBING MODERN GARDEN ROSES
Non-recurrent ground cover
Recurrent ground cover
Non-recurrent shrub
Recurrent shrub
Recurrent bush
   Large-flowered bush
   Cluster-flowered bush
   Polyantha
Recurrent miniature

● CLIMBING MODERN GARDEN ROSE
Non-recurrent rambler
Non-recurrent climber
Non-recurrent climbing miniature
Recurrent rambler
Recurrent climber
Recurrent climbing miniature

Old garden roses

● NON-CLIMBING OLD GARDEN ROSES
Alba
Bourbon
China
Damask
Gallica
Hybrid perpetual
Moss
Portland
Provence (centifolia)
Sweet briar
Tea

● CLIMBING OLD GARDEN ROSES
Ayrshire
Boursalt
Climbing tea
Noisette
Sempervirens

Wild roses

Non-climbing wild roses
Climbing roses

79

◄ 'Valencia' is a modern Hybrid tea with pure apricot flowers and a delightful fragrance with disease-resistant foliage.

► Many of the *Rugosas* are extensively used for amenity planting where their ruggedness is equal to urban environments.

▼ The Times Rose is a fine example of an extremely healthy modern Floribunda with the bonus of bronze-red foliage.

► Far right: 'Red Ace', in association with other miniature roses, can provide a pleasing mixture of colour in a small border.

Fig. 24 Flower heads.

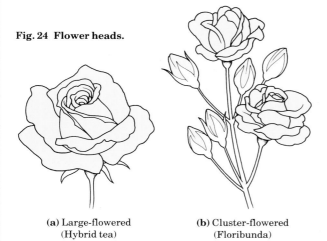

(a) Large-flowered
(Hybrid tea)

(b) Cluster-flowered
(Floribunda)

Fig. 25 Flower shapes (number of petals).

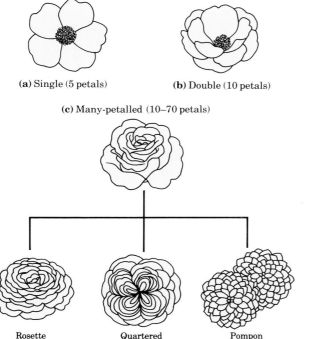

(a) Single (5 petals)　　　(b) Double (10 petals)

(c) Many-petalled (10–70 petals)

Rosette　　　Quartered　　　Pompon

FLORIBUNDA BUSH ROSES

Relative to the history of the rose, the Floribundas are newcomers. In the last 50 years their popularity and colour has equalled their older cousins. Because of their tremendous difference in height, special attention has been made of this characteristic where important. The majority in this select list are ideal to provide large splashes of colour.

Name	Description
Amber Queen	An extremely healthy amber with perfectly formed flowers.
Anna Livia	A fragrant pink with a nice length of stem for cutting.
Arthur Bell	A tall bright yellow fading to cream with a pleasing fragrance.
Beautiful Britain	Tomato red with large clusters of medium sized flowers.
Bonfire Night	Yellow clusters turning red as they age. Dark green foliage.
Brown Velvet	A complete colour break. The russet-brown blooms are freely produced.
Bucks Fizz	A clear soft orange with fragrance, useful tall bedder or cut flower.
Christopher Columbus	Semi-double small blooms striped crimson and pale pink.
City of Leeds	Salmon-pink clusters of medium sized blooms, good for showing.
English Miss	Light rose-pink clusters with a good fragrance.
Evening Star	Large flowers of pure creamy white on a medium to tall plant.
Fragrant Delight	Light orange-red. Huge trusses of scented blooms.
Hannah Gordon	White edged pink. A robust grower with glossy deep green foliage.
Harvest Fayre	Pure pastel apricot double blooms which performs particularly well in the autumn.
Iceberg	The most continuous-flowering Floribunda ever bred. Pure white clusters on a tall plant.

Korresia	The most successful yellow Floribunda to date with a delightful scent and healthy foliage.
Many Happy Returns	A pretty bush that can be grown in beds and containers. A light rosy blush.
Margaret Merrill	White with a hint of pink. A very fragrant sturdy bush.
Masquerade	The original variety to start yellow turning pink and red as it ages. Requires dead heading to maintain a continuity of flower.
Matangi	Bright orange-red blooms with a white eye. Upright, medium-sized.
Memento	Large clusters of salmon vermilion which is very free flowering.
Mountbatten	Large double-scented blooms of mimosa yellow. Vigorous, makes a good specimen plant.
Princess Michael	Large well-shaped blooms of canary yellow on a robust bush with a pleasing fragrance.
Sea Pearl	A tall bush of beautifully shaped blooms of salmon pink. The long stems are ideal for cutting and last well in water.
Sexy Rexy	Medium to light pink with amazing clusters of perfectly formed medium-sized flowers.
Sheila's Perfume	A lovely scented and blush red bi-colour. The dark green foliage is a perfect foil.
Southampton	A beautifully scented apricot-orange. Tall and free flowering with a pleasing fragrance.
Sue Lawley	Carmine pink and white. A novel mixture of colours giving an intriguingly pretty cluster.
Tango	Orange blooms tipped with pale yellow. A novelty with great appeal.
The Queen Elizabeth Rose	A very tall robust grower with cyclamen pink blooms. Useful as a specimen bush or hedge. Good for cutting.
The Times Rose	A perfect medium-sized bush. The dark green disease free foliage is a fantastic foil for the deep crimson red clusters.
Trumpeter	Bright scarlet. The short bushy plant is full of flower and luminous.

· SYNONYMS ·

Many roses of international repute are catalogued in the major rose-growing countries. They may however have different names, depending on the country they are being sold in. This is a selection of the more widely grown varieties that possess synonyms.

Common name	Alternative name
Angela Rippon	Ocarina
Anna Livia	Trier 2000
Blue Moon	Mainzer Fasnacht
Chilterns	Mainaufeuer
Congratulations	Sylvia
Elina	Peaudouce
Evelyn Fison	Irish Wonder
Flower Carpet	Heidetraum
Fragrant Cloud	Duftwolke
Grouse	Immensee
Iceberg	Schneewitchen
Keepsake	Esmeralda
Kent	White Cover
Korresia	Fresia/Sunsprite
Loving Memory	Burgund 81
Margaret Thatcher	Flamingo
Miss Pam Ayres	Bonanza
Peace	Gloria Dei
Penelope Keith	Freegold
Perestroika	Sonnenkind
Pheasant	Heidekonigen
Regensberg	Young Mistress
Royal William	Duftsauber 84
Savoy Hotel	Integrity
Selfridges	Berolina
Simba	Helmut Schmidt
Suffolk	Bassino
Super Star	Tropicana
Sweet Promise	Sonia
Tango	Stretch Johnson
Tequila Sunrise	Beaulieu
Troika	Royal Dane

GROUND-COVER ROSES

Ground-cover roses vary tremendously in their size and plant form. It is therefore convenient to divide them into groups relative to these criteria.

Prostrate growers for the small garden

Name	Colour
Avon	White
Gwent	Yellow
Hampshire	Scarlet
Nozomi	Pearl pink
Snow Carpet	White
Suffolk	Scarlet
Swany	White

Prostrate growers for the bigger garden

Chilterns	Deep crimson
Flower Carpet	Bright pink
Grouse	Pale pink
Pheasant	Rose pink
Pink Drift	Pink
Red Max Graf	Scarlet
Scarlet Meidiland	Orange-red
White Max Graf	Pure white

Arching growers for the small garden

Kent	White
Northamptonshire	Flesh pink
Surrey	Soft pink
The Fairy	Soft pink

Arching growers for the bigger garden

Bonica	Pale pink
Eye Opener	Red
Ferdy	Fuchsia pink
Fiona	Blood red
Pink Bells	Soft pink
Pink Chimo	Pink
Pink Wave	Satin pink
Red Blanket	Rose red
Red Rascal	Red
Rosy Cushion	Rosy pink
Smarty	Rose madder
Tall Story	Pale primrose
White Bells	White

PATIO ROSES

Name	Colour
Anna Ford	Deep orange
Bright Smile	Yellow
Buttons	Light salmon red
Clarissa	Scarlet
Chelsea Pensioner	Scarlet
City Lights	Yellow
Cider Cup	Deep apricot
Emily Louise	Yellow
Gentle Touch	Pale pink
Golden Rosamini	Golden yellow
Hakuun	Cream
Little Bo Peep	Pale pink
Longleat	Red
Mandarin	Orange and yellow
Peek a Boo	Apricot pink
Penelope Keith	Deep yellow and gold
Perestroika	Yellow
Pretty Polly	Soft pink
Queen Mother	Soft pink
Red Minimo	Red
Rosy Future	Rose pink
Rugul	Yellow
Sweet Dream	Peach apricot
Sweet Magic	Orange and gold
Tear Drop	White
Valois Rose	Creamy yellow and cerise

MINIATURE ROSES

Name	Colour
Baby Sunrise	Copper apricot
Baby Masquerade	Yellow and red
Darling Flame	Yellow and vermilion
Green Diamond	Greenish white
Easter Morning	Ivory
Magic Carousel	White tipped pink
Pour Toi	Creamy white
Red Ace	Dark crimson
Royal Salute	Rose red
Starina	Orange red
Stacey Sue	Light pink

◄ 'Memento' is a tremendously free-flowering salmon-red Floribunda with a good health record and is useful as a cut flower variety.

◄ Below: 'Ballerina', a medium-sized shrub rose which has a long flowering period. The large mop heads of light pink blooms with white centres are reminiscent of phlox.

▼ Standard 'Nozomi' is a prime example of a ground cover plant that can be adapted to make a superb contribution to the garden in this style.

CLIMBERS AND RAMBLERS

Scented

The best recurrent climbers

Name	Colour
Altissimo	Bright red
Bantry Bay	Pink
Compassion*	Pink/apricot
Danse de Feu	Orange scarlet
Dreaming Spires*	Golden yellow
Dublin Bay	Bright crimson
Golden Showers	Bright yellow
Handel	Cream flushed rose-pink
Laura Ford	Yellow amber
Malaga*	Rose pink
Madame Alfred Carrière*	White
Mermaid	Sulphur yellow
Parade	Carmine red
Pink Perpétue	Carmine pink
Schoolgirl*	Apricot
Souvenir de Claudius Denoyel*	Crimson
Summer Wine	Deep pink
Sympathie	Deep red
The New Dawn*	Pearl pink
Warm Welcome	Orange vermilion
Zéphirine Drouhin*	Carmine pink

The best summer-flowering climbers and ramblers

Albéric Barbier	Cream
Albertine*	Salmon and pink
American Pillar	Carmine/white eye
Bobby James*	Creamy white
Cécile Brunner (Climber)	Light pink
Iceberg (Climber)	White
Crimson Shower	Crimson
Emily Gray	Chamois-yellow
Félicité et Perpétue	White
R. filipes Kiftsgate*	Creamy white
Francois Juranville	Salmon pink
Maigold*	Apricot-yellow
Paul's Scarlet	Bright scarlet
The Garland*	Blush
Wedding Day*	Cream

Roses for pillars and walls

Aloha*	Rose and salmon-pink
Bantry Bay	Pink
Compassion	Pink shaded apricot
Dublin Bay	Bright crimson
Golden Showers	Bright yellow
Handel	Cream flushed rose-pink
Phyllis Bide	Light yellow and pink
Sympathie	Deep red
White Cockade	White
Zéphirine Drouhin	Pale rose-pink

Roses for pergolas

Albéric Barbier	Cream
Albertine	Salmon
Bobby James	Creamy white
Cécile Brunner (Climber)	Pink
Iceberg (Climber)	White
Crimson Shower	Scarlet
François Juranville	Salmon-pink
Paul's Scarlet	Bright scarlet
Rambling Rector	White
Summer Wine	Pink
Vielchenblau	Pale lilac
Wedding Day	Cream

· GROWING ROSES INTO TREES ·

To do this successfully requires patience but will produce the most remarkable profusions of colour. Because the soil is generally of a poor quality in these situations care must be taken to prepare the planting position with extra attention adding a plentiful supply of good organic compost. The planting position should be in full sun. Keep the young shoots well tied in.   *Very fragrant*

Name	Colour
Albertine*	Salmon pink
Bobbie James	White
Kiftsgate*	Creamy white
R. longicuspis	White
Paul's Himalayan Musk*	Pink/lavender
Rambling Rector	Creamy white
The Garland	Pale pink
Wedding Day*	White-yellow

MODERN SHRUB ROSES

Name	Colour
Ballerina	Light pink
Buff Beauty	Apricot buff
Cerise Bouquet*	Cherry red
Constance Spry*	Rose pink
Cornelia	Rich salmon pink
Felicia	Shell pink
Fred Loads	Vermilion orange
Fritz Nobis*	Rose pink
Fruhlingsgold*	Primrose yellow
Fruhlingsmorgen*	Pink yellow base
Golden Wings	Light yellow
Graham Thomas	Yellow
Heritage	Shell pink
Kathleen Ferrier	Salmon pink
Kordes Robusta	Crimson red
Marjorie Fair	Carmine white eye
Marguerite Hilling*	Pink
Mary Hayley Bell	Dark pink
Miss Pam Ayres	Yellow and red
Nevada*	Creamy white
Penelope	Pale salmon pink
Red Dot	Red
The Seckford Rose	Glowing pink
Westerland	Golden orange
Yesterday	Magenta rose

* Very large shrubs that are showy but only summer flowering.

Shrub roses grown as single specimens

Blanc Double de Coubert	White
Buff Beauty	Light apricot
Felicia	Light pink
Fruhlingsgold	Primrose-yellow
R. moyesii 'Geranium'	Bright crimson
Golden Wings	Light yellow
Marguerite Hilling	Pink
Nevada	Cream
Penelope	Creamy pink
Robusta	Scarlet
R. omeiensis pteracantha	White
Roseraie de l'Haÿ	Claret

Climbers grown as shrubs

These are many of the modern climbers that make splendid shrubs. All are recurrent. This type of plant will give height to the back of the border and provide splashes of colour in mid-summer. They require very little maintenance other than heavy deadheading.

Aloha	Coral pink
Altissimo	Bright red
Compassion	Salmon shaded orange
Danse de Feu	Orange red
Dublin Bay	Deep red
Golden Showers	Bright yellow
Handel	Creamy white and pink
Joseph's Coat	Yellow-orange and red
Laura Ford	Yellow-amber
Warm Welcome	Orange vermilion
White Cockade	White

· ROSES FOR SHADE ·

Growing roses in the shade can be very difficult, particularly on north or east walls. However it is not impossible and there are a wide range of ramblers and climbers that will give a modest return to the ambitious gardener. Do not expect the same quantity of flower that will be produced on a southerly aspect, but the following varieties will give much satisfaction. **Very fragrant*

Name	Colour
Aloha*	Coral pink
Danse de Feu	Orange red
Dortmund	Red with a white centre
Gloire de Dijon*	Buff yellow
Golden Showers	Bright yellow
Kathleen Harrop*	Pale pink
Maigold*	Bronze yellow
Mermaid	Sulphur yellow
Madame Alfred Carrière*	White
Parade	Deep pink
Sympathie	Bright scarlet
The New Dawn*	Flesh pink
Zéphirine Drouhin*	Carmine pink

OLD-FASHIONED ROSES (HERITAGE ROSES)

A select list of the favourites before the modern rose, which will give immense pleasure in the early summer. The majority are lax shrubs requiring little maintenance.

Series	Name	Colour
Alba	Great Maiden's Blush	Creamy pink
	Maxima	White
Bourbon	Boule de Neige	Pure white
	Honorine de Brabant	Pink striped lilac

Bourbon (continued)	La Reine Victoria	Deep pink
	Louise Odier	Rich pink
	Madame Isaac Pereire	Rose pink
	Madame Pierre Oger	Cream reversed rose
	Souvenir de la Malmaison	Blush pink
	Variegata de Bologna	White striped purple
Centifolia	Fantin Latour	Pale pink
	Rose de Meaux	Light pink
	Tour de Malakoff	Magenta
China	Cécile Brunner	Flesh pink
	Hermosa	Pink
	Old Blush	Pink
Damask	Ispahan	Pink
	Kazanlik	Deep pink
	Madame Hardy	Pure white
	York and Lancaster	Pale pink and white
Gallica	Camaieux	Soft rose pink
	Cardinal Richelieu	Rich amethyst
	Charles de Mills	Crimson maroon
	Rosa Mundi	Crimson/white striped
	Tuscany Superb	Crimson purple
Hybrid Perpetual	Baron Girod de l'Ain	Crimson and white
	Ferdinand Pichard	Pink streaked crimson
	Gloire de Ducher	Crimson purple
	Paul Neyron	Pale rose-pink
	Reine des Violettes	Lilac purple
	Roger Lambelin	Crimson tipped white
	Souvenir de Dr Jamain	Damson purple
Moss	Common Moss	Rose pink
	Nuits de Young	Deep purple
	White Moss	Pure white
	William Lobb	Crimson purple
Rugosa	Blanc Double de Coubert	White
	Roseraie de l'Haÿ	Crimson purple

▲ 'Dame Wendy', an unusually fragrant pink Floribunda with a pleasing bushy habit and glossy dark green foliage.

▶ 'Lovers' Meeting', a Hybrid tea with bright reddish-orange blooms that will create a startling splash of colour in the garden and has deep bronzy foliage.

◀ 'Wishing', a deep salmon Floribunda with medium-sized flowers which are borne in small clusters and will also make very useful decorative material.

SPECIES (WILD ROSES)

The specie roses from which all our modern varieties evolved from. Allowed to grow naturally, they can give colour and variety to many situations in the garden.

Name	Colour
R. ecae var. 'Helen Knight'	Golden yellow
R. farreri persetosa[2]	Soft pink
R. forrestiana[1]	Pink
R. gallica complicata	Bright pink
R. highdownensis[1]	Deep pink
R. hugonis	Soft yellow
R. gallica officinalis	Red
R. macrophylla[1]	Pink
R. mirifica stellata	Rose purple
R. moyesii[1]	Metallic red
R. moyesii var. Geranium[1]	Geranium-red
R. moyesii holodonta[1]	Pink
R. nitida[2]	Pink
R. omiensis pteracantha[2]	White
R. pomifera[1]	Bright pink
R. primula[2,3]	Pale yellow
R. roxburghii	Pale pink
R. rubiginosa[3]	Pink
R. rubrifolia (R. glauca)[2,1]	Pink
R. rugosa alba[1]	White
R. rugosa rubra[1]	Claret
R. soulieana	White
R. spinossisima	Pink or white
R. sweginzowii[1]	Rose pink
R. virginiana[2]	Bright pink
R. willmottiae[2]	Mauve pink
R. webbiana[1]	Pale pink
R. woodsii fendlerii[1]	Lilac pink
R. xanthina var. 'Canary Bird'	Golden yellow

Fig. 26 Thorns.

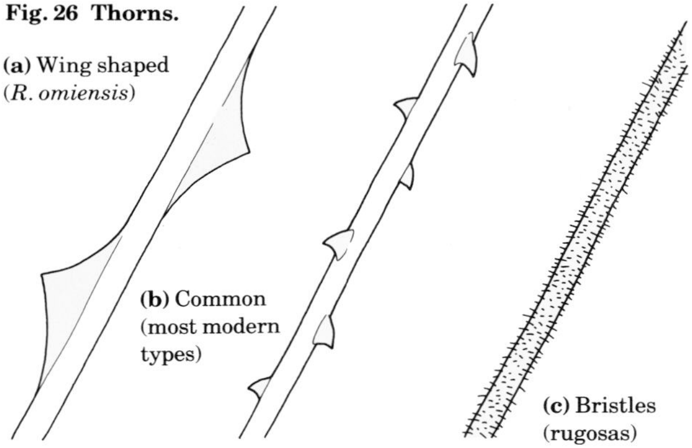

(a) Wing shaped (*R. omiensis*)

(b) Common (most modern types)

(c) Bristles (rugosas)

Fig. 27 Hips.

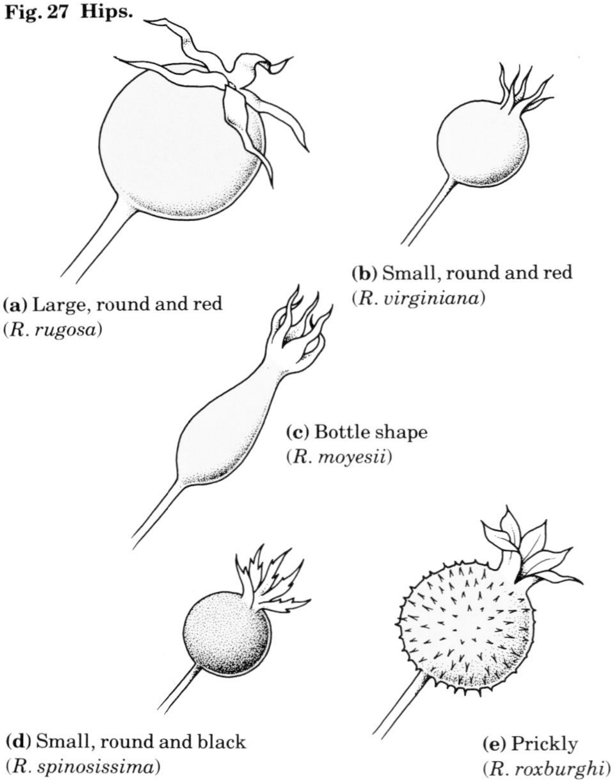

(a) Large, round and red (*R. rugosa*)

(b) Small, round and red (*R. virginiana*)

(c) Bottle shape (*R. moyesii*)

(d) Small, round and black (*R. spinosissima*)

(e) Prickly (*R. roxburghi*)

[1] *Decorative hips;* [2] *Decorative foliage;* [3] *Scented foliage*

STANDARD ROSES

A selection of varieties which will produce good heads of bloom on a well-proportioned and balanced plant. Standard roses are usually determined by the measurement taken from ground level to the first arm that has been propagated. The generally accepted measuremens are given in brackets.

Hybrid teas (100cm/3¼ ft)

Name	Colour
Alec's Red	Deep red
Blessings	Coral salmon
Loving Memory	Crimson scarlet
Peace	Canary yellow and pink
Remember Me	Coppery-orange
Silver Jubilee	Apricot-pink and cream
Simba	Pure yellow

Floribundas (100cm/3¼ ft)

Amber Queen	Amber yellow
Anna Livia	Pink
Iceberg	Pure white
Margaret Merrill	Blush white
The Times Rose	Crimson scarlet

Half-standards (patio roses) (75cm/2½ ft)

Gentle Touch	Pale pink
Sweet Magic	Orange and gold

Shrub standards (120cm/4ft)

Ballerina	Pink with a white eye
Chilterns	Crimson
Flower Carpet	Bright pink
Nozomi	Pale pink
The Fairy	Pink
Surrey	Soft pink
Canary Bird	Yellow

Weeping standards (umbrella roses) (150cm/5ft)

Alberic Barbier	Pale yellow
Crimson Shower	Crimson
Dorothy Perkins	Rose-pink
Francois Juranville	Salmon pink

ROSES FOR FLORAL ART

Although all roses look pretty when used for decorative purposes there are many that do not appear to last long when cut. This is technically called failing to take up water. There are in the garden many varieties which naturally have a good length of stem and are by this criteria easier to cut. This is a selection of garden roses that are good for cutting.

Name	Colour
Alexander	Vermilion
Anna Livia	Pink
Ann Harkness	Apricot
Apricot Silk	Orange red
Arthur Bell	Bright yellow
Blue Moon	Lilac pink
Brown Velvet	Russet brown
Bucks Fizz	Soft orange
Congratulations	Soft pink and salmon
Julia's Rose	Tan
Loving Memory	Dark red
Memento	Salmon red
National Trust	Bright red
Pascali	White
Pink Pearl	Pearl
Sea Pearl	Shell pink and pearl
Selfridges	Bright yellow
Tango	Orange and yellow
The Queen Elizabeth Rose	Clear pink
The Times Rose	Crimson scarlet
Woods of Windsor	Deep pink and apricot

In addition to this list there are of course many varieties available from florists. These have been specifically bred to give high yielding results in greenhouses, an ability to travel and give lasting satisfaction to the recipients. (The majority of these varieties will not make good garden roses.)

Whatever the source, cut flowers will last for a very long time if they are cut in the cool and stood in plenty of treated water before arranging.

Appendix

SOCIETIES AND FURTHER INFORMATION

The novice gardener will not want for advice. Everybody with an interest in horticulture will freely guide the beginner in the right direction. Most countries have societies which publish magazines, hold shows and run lectures; some have big gardens. In the rose-growing world there is an abundance of these societies which can be most helpful. The biggest is in the UK, the Royal National Rose Society, but many countries have their own groups or clubs. This is a selection from some of the members of the World Federation of Rose Societies.

UK
The Royal National Rose Society
Chiswell Green, St Albans
Hertfordshire AL2 3NR, England

For those enthusiasts who aspire to breeding roses as an absorbing hobby they will be well advised to join: The Amateur Rose Breeders' Association, 48 Shrewsbury Fields, Shifnal, Shropshire TF11 8AN, England.

Argentina
The Rose Society of Argentina,
Av. Quintana 576, 1129 Buenos Aires

Australia
The National Rose Society of Australia
271b Belmore Road, North Balwyn
Victoria 3104

Belgium
Société Royale Nationale
'Les Amis de la Rose'
Kalverhage 3, B-9230 Melle

Bermuda
The Bermuda Rose Society
PO Box PG 162, Paget PG BX

Canada
The Canadian Rose Society
10 Fairfax Crescent, Scarborough
Ontario M1L 1Z8

France
Société Française des Roses
6 rue J.B. Couty, 69009 Lyon

Germany
Verein Deutscher Rosenfreunde
Waldstrasse 14
7570 Baden-Baden

India
The Indian Rose Federation
'Saurabh', 4-A Narbada Road
Jabalpur-482001 (MP)

Israel
Wohl Rose Park
PO Box 1312, Jerusalem

Italy
Associazione Italiana della Rosa
Via Missori 8, 20052 Monza (MI)

Japan
Japan Rose Society
3–9–5 Oyamadai, Setagaya-ku
Tokyo 158

Netherlands
Nederlandse Rozenvereniging
Heidelaan 8, 9301 KJ Roden

New Zealand
National Rose Society of New
    Zealand Inc.
PO Box 66, Bunnythorpe
Palmerston North

Northern Ireland
The Rose Society of Northern Ireland
10 Eastleigh Drive
Belfast BT4 3DX

Pakistan
Pakistan National Rose Society
Plot No. 395–396, Sector 1/9
Industrial Area, Islamabad

South Africa
Federation of Rose Societies of
    South Africa
5 Douglas Street, Wavarley
Johannesburg 2090

Spain
Asociación Española de la Rosa
Parque del Oeste
Rosaleda Ramon Ortiz
28008 Madrid

▶ **The Royal National Rose Society in liaison with the British Association Representing Breeders stages a group of the newest introductions at the Chelsea Flower Show every year.**

Switzerland
Geselleschaft Schweizerischer
   Rosenfreunde
Banhofstr 11, CH–8640 Rapperswill

Uruguay
Asociación Uruguaya de la Rosa
Cavia 3099–Apt. 11, 11300 Montevideo

USA
American Rose Society
PO Box 30,000
Shreveport, LA 71130

ROSE GARDENS TO VISIT

The most universally admired garden plant is the centre of attraction in many of the world's most famous gardens. Each of these is an expression of the county or country in which it is situated.

UK

Mottisfont Abbey, Romsey, Hampshire
The national collection of old garden roses is cleverly associated with shrubs and herbaceous material.

RHS Garden, Wisley, Surrey
A tremendous diversity of garden plants, a mecca for all horticulturalists.

RNRS Gardens of the Rose, St Albans, Hertfordshire
A magnificent garden at the headquarters of the Royal National Rose Society incorporating the new seedling rose trials.

Sir Thomas and Lady Dixon Park
Belfast, Northern Ireland
An historic rose garden, part of a splendid rose park which was completely redesigned for the World Rose Conference in 1992.

Eire

St Annes Park, Dublin
Huge beds of modern varieties and an exquisite patio and miniature rose garden.

France

Parc de la Tete d'Or, Lyons
One of the world's great rose gardens with vast areas of modern roses, reputed to total some 100,000 bushes.

Roserie du Parc du Bagatelle, Paris
Pergolas and arches are but part of a superb rose garden which also incorporates a new rose trial.

Germany

Insel Mainau, Lake Constance
A dream garden on an island in Lake Constance with a large area devoted to growing roses as shrubs.

Westfalenpark, Dortmund
A large collection of new and old varieties with each recognized breeder represented in individual pots.

Zweibrucken City Rose Garden
Near Saarbrucken
Recently redesigned Rose Garden, incorporating a fascinating compilation of garden architecture, plants and water features.

Australia
Royal Botanic Gardens
South Yarah, Victoria
A blend of the old and new planted with considerable expertise and enthusiasm.

Switzerland
Parc de la Grange, Geneva
The garden on the south side of Lake Leman is an intriguing blend of new and the not-so-new varieties.

Italy
Municipal Rose Garden, Rome
A wonderful display of climbing, rambling and bush roses in a natural amphitheatre near the ruins of the Palace of the Caesars.

Holland
Westbroekpark, The Hague
A tremendous collection of modern roses beautifully laid out which forms the basis of the most famous rose trials in Europe.

Spain
Parque del Oeste, Madrid
For the sheer beauty of its rambling roses this garden has few rivals.

USA

American Rose Centre
Shreveport, Louisiana
The American Rose Society has constructed an imaginative garden to celebrate its 100th anniversary.

Hershey Rose Garden, Pennsylvania
An interesting display of modern bush and shrub roses sited in a rolling park.

Huntington Botanical Gardens
San Marino, California
A fabulous garden that boasts a tropical input and a famous botanical library.

USEFUL PUBLICATIONS
Such is the proliferation of rose varieties it is helpful to know if one can find a source without embarking on an expensive catalogue research programme. Fortunately there are two publications which are invaluable in this respect.

Find That Rose published by the British Rose Growers Association lists some 2,600 varieties which are obtainable in the UK with sources. Copies may be obtained from: British Rose Growers Association, 303 Mile End Road, Colchester, Essex CO4 5EA.

The Combined Rose List is an American publication which gives much the same information as *Find That Rose*, but on an international scale with some 7,000 varieties; 87 sources in the States and Canada and over 100 worldwide. Copies may be obtained from: Peter Schneider, PO Box 16035, Rocky River, OH 44116, USA.

Index

Page numbers in *italics* indicate an illustration or boxed table.